PRLA

BoB. 14006
416181

KHAN, V.S. (ed).
Minority families in Britain
CENTRAL

- -

Charges are payable on books overdue at public libraries. This book is
due for return by the last date shown but if not required by another
reader may be renewed — ask at the library, telephone or write
quoting the last date and the details shown above.

Studies in Ethnicity
In association with the Social Science Research Council

Editorial board
Professor Michael Banton, Professor Percy Cohen,
Dr Sandra Wallman

'Studies in Ethnicity' emerges out of the work of the Social Science Research Council (SSRC) Research Unit in Ethnic Relations, whether directly or indirectly. It treats ethnicity as both an empirical and a conceptual problem, reporting new studies in ethnic relations and new approaches to the study of ethnicity.

The first titles in the series are:

Sandra Wallman (ed.): *Ethnicity at Work*

Verity Saifullah Khan (ed.): *Minority Families in Britain*

Minority Families in Britain

Support and Stress

Edited by

Verity Saifullah Khan

First published 1979 by
THE MACMILLAN PRESS LTD
London and Basingstoke
Associated companies in Delhi Dublin
Hong Kong Johannesburg Lagos Melbourne
New York Singapore and Tokyo

Phototypeset in V.I.P. Baskerville by
Western Printing Services Ltd, Bristol
Printed in Great Britain by Lowe and
Brydone Printers Ltd, Thetford, Norfolk

British Library Cataloguing in Publication Data

Minority families in Britain. – (Studies in ethnicity).
   1. Family – Great Britain   2. Minorities – Great
   Britain   3. Welfare work with minorities – Great
   Britain   4. Family social work – Great Britain
   I. Saifullah Khan, Verity   II. Series
   301.45′1′0941   HQ614

   ISBN 0–333–26189–5
   ISBN 0–333–26190–9   Pbk

Contents

Notes on Contributors

CATHERINE BALLARD read Anglo-Saxon and Norse at the University of Cambridge, worked in India and from 1971 to 1975 was a Research Associate at the SSRC Research Unit on Ethnic Relations at the University of Bristol. She is currently lecturing on Indian and Pakistani minorities in Britain.

ROGER BALLARD read Social Anthropology at the University of Cambridge. From 1966 to 1968 he did his doctoral research, in a village in the Himalayan foothills, from the University of Delhi. From 1970 to 1975 he was a Research Associate at the SSRC Research Unit on Ethnic Relations at the University of Bristol. During this period he and Catherine Ballard carried out field research in Leeds and the Punjab, India. He was appointed Research Lecturer in Race Relations at the University of Leeds in 1975.

GEOFFREY DRIVER is Visiting Fellow in Race Relations at the University of Bradford. He studied at the University of Nottingham (BA) and at the University of Illinois (MA, Ph D). From 1969 to 1970 he was a research worker at the Bureau of Educational Research, University of Illinois; from 1971 to 1972 he was a teacher in the Social Education Department, William Milliam Murdoch Secondary School, Birmingham; and from 1972 to 1976 he was Senior Lecturer in Sociology of Education, St Peter's College, Birmingham.

ESTHER GOODY is Lecturer in Social Anthropology at Newhall College, University of Cambridge. She has worked mainly in West Africa, especially among the Gonja of Northern Ghana.

CHRISTINE GROOTHUES (née MUIR) graduated in Social Anthropology from the University of Cambridge, and has a Diploma in Social Administration from the London School of Economics. She worked as a Child Care Officer for the London Borough of Southwark for two years before participating in a research project on West Africans in London. Since then she has spent two years in Accra, Ghana, studying child care and development and on her return has worked as a social worker for the Commonwealth Students' Children Society in London.

ROBIN OAKLEY is a Lecturer in Sociology at Bedford College, University of London. His main interests include the sociology of race, ethnicity, migration and comparative sociology. He is editor of *New Backgrounds: the Immigrant Child at Home and at School* (1968).

PHILIP RACK has been Consultant Psychiatrist at Lynfield Mount Hospital since 1967 and has taken particular interest in the psychiatric problems of immigrants in the last five years. He is a member of the United Kingdom Committee of the World Federation for Mental Health, Vice-Chairman of Bradford Community Relations Council, and one of the people who has drawn the attention of psychiatrists to the importance of Transcultural Psychiatry. He was the organiser of the International Congress on Transcultural Psychiatry held in Bradford, Yorkshire, in July 1976, from which many of the papers in this volume have arisen.

VERITY SAIFULLAH KHAN is a Research Associate at the SSRC Research Unit on Ethnic Relations at the University of Bristol. She is a social anthropologist. Her doctoral research is on Pakistani (Mirpuri) villagers in Bradford and involved research in Mirpur, Pakistan, in 1972 and 1973. Her present research project, entitled 'Asian Women and Work', is part of the work of a team studying 'Ethnicity and Work' in South London.

PETER WEINREICH is Principal Lecturer in the Department of Psychology at Ulster College. From 1970 to 1977 he was a Programme Leader at the SSRC Research Unit on Ethnic Relations at the University of Bristol. He has devised an approach for the study of self-concept development in adolescents in a multi-ethnic context and generated a programme of research of which his chapter in this volume reports one aspect.

Preface

The origin of this volume was a conference held in July 1976 in Bradford, Yorkshire, entitled the International Congress on Transcultural Psychiatry. Besides the impressive names and numbers of psychiatrists, pharmacologists and doctors, the conference brought together a small group of anthropologists, sociologists and social psychologists who work among ethnic minorities in Britain. Our contribution to the very concrete and specific difficulties faced by psychiatrists and doctors was clear and daunting. We decided that some of the papers presented could form the basis of a volume (C. Ballard, R. Ballard, Saifullah Khan and Weinreich). The organiser of the conference, Dr Philip Rack, kindly supported the plan and contributed his own paper. Further papers were sought to extend our subject matter. One was chosen from a conference on family processes held at the SSRC Research Unit on Ethnic Relations at the University of Bristol in early 1977 (Goody). This conference in Bristol provided a further example of the need for a dialogue between academics and practitioners. The impatience that was developing among the latter was for research directly relevant to their problems and interests, and research that was understandable to themselves and other, less involved colleagues. Two other authors were then asked to rewrite existing work for the volume (Oakley, Driver).

Each of the eight papers in the volume considers a particular minority and/or a section of a statutory service which provides a 'service' for minority members. There is a general progression through the volume from those papers focusing on the internal workings of ethnic minorities (first generation and then second generation) to those that look at the relationship between different statutory services and ethnic minorities. Most of the papers focus on either support or stress at one of the levels outlined in the introduction.

The papers were written by authors of various disciplines – some academic, some practical – and each has branched out beyond the usual confines of his or her sphere of enquiry. It is these two charac-teristics – the multidisciplinary and applied approach – of the volume which are its distinctive contribution, but they also present added editorial difficulties. However, as indicated at the beginning of the introduction, whatever the weaknesses and difficulties involved, the contributors are determined to point to the strengths and contribu-tion of the exercise.

In this spirit, it is constructive to preface this volume by mentioning a few of the particular problems faced by its editor and contributors. The multidisciplinary nature of the volume and its intention to be readable to a wide variety of practitioners demanded the minimum of complex terminology, and the use of simple concepts that would incorporate the various meanings and the dynamics of the situations under consideration. Hence the notions of support and stress, which all readers can use to examine not only their particular area of work, but also their own lives and relationship with the statutory services.

Academics as well as practitioners may face the serious and deli-cate problem of upholding the confidentiality of informants. This involves disguising the real identity of informants by the use of pseudonyms, but also has, in certain papers, necessitated the use of composite quotes or case studies. This problem and certain other ethical issues are confounded in this field of enquiry by the possible unintended repercussions of publishing findings which can prove not only personally embarrassing for the persons or populations con-cerned, but also politically dangerous. Several contributors to this volume have suffered from distortions of their work and findings by the popular press. The most straightforward analysis of situations presented with the intention of improving mutual understanding and putting forward a minority viewpoint can produce, through such intervention, the opposite effect. While breaking the trust and confi-dence between author and informants, the information may, more seriously, be used in support of arguments and activities working to undermine the fundamental rights of members of minorities, and to exacerbate the degree of hostility between different communities. These problems have led some of the contributors (although not in the case of this volume) to delay publication of material or to seek publication in a more obscure journal or volume so that it will be less accessible to the 'real' world.

This question may overestimate the influence that social scientists, researchers and practitioners have on the present ethnic relations situation. However, they do indicate very real dilemmas and processes which tend to inhibit communication between practitioners/researchers and minorities, and between researchers and practitioners.

A final example emerged from the question of the categories and labels used to distinguish minority groups. This led to a lot of debate and no clear-cut agreement between contributors. But many of us agree that the categories used by the society at large do not reflect the diversity of existing populations, nor do they correspond to the people's own classification of themselves. We argue, therefore, that where differences exist and specificity and understanding are the aims, social scientists, social workers and others should not reinforce popular misconceptions by using general labels such as 'West Indian' or 'Asian' or even 'Cypriot', even though it may seem to some to be politically expedient. However, this volume addresses itself expressly to many people who use such general categories. Certain contributors felt this to be a justification for the use of general terms as it would facilitate communication, whereas others saw it to be an opportunity to 'put the picture straight'. For others the nature of the research and its setting determined the categories chosen. Each contributor has, therefore, chosen his/her own stance and specified the type and focus of the research undertaken.

I am most grateful to the contributors for allowing their papers to be published in this volume. Ultimate responsibility for the volume is my own and the views presented are not those of the Social Science Research Council nor necessarily those of the SSRC's Research Unit on Ethnic Relations.

V.S.K.

Introduction[1]

Verity Saifullah Khan

This volume is exploratory. It stands as a determined statement by the contributors of the need to move beyond their traditional professional preserves. All the contributors have worked either with members of ethnic minorities or with social, educational or medical practitioners who work among various minorities. All are keen to share their knowledge and insight with workers who are daily in touch with, and often make decisions on behalf of, members of ethnic minorities. While presenting new information on ethnic minorities, the volume is also a statement in support of opening up a dialogue between the researcher and the practitioner and facilitating communication between academic and professionals in various fields. This is an objective often thwarted by professional chauvinism and the lack of channels for communication and co-operative action. It is hoped, however, that this volume and the spirit that initiated it will stimulate others both within the minorities and among policy-makers in positions of influence to contribute to this important field of action and enquiry.

The support and stress of the title refer to the support and stress experienced by members of ethnic minorities and workers in the statutory services in Britain alike. By connecting ethnic minorities with the educational, social and medical services in this way, it is possible to reject the perspective that typifies minorities as the source of all problems, both their own and those of the majority society, and the statutory services as the only means of help and support. The papers in this volume describe reservoirs of support within ethnic minorities which are rarely tapped or encouraged by those outside; and they point to difficulties faced by the 'helping' agencies which hinder their effectiveness as supportive services for certain sections of the population.

In real life these fields overlap. Members of ethnic minorities do use, and are influenced by, the statutory services and the services themselves are aware of, and influenced by, culture and communication difficulties characteristic of particular groups. The extent of contact and take-up differ markedly within any one minority, between minorities and between the various services. In times of crisis many people turn to friends, family or kin before considering the relevant statutory service. Some populations, however, are reluctant to consider 'outside' forms of help and some have limited personal resources available to them. In certain instances traditional systems of support, such as the herbalist doctor or 'the church', will prove more effective, yet in others they will complicate or delay the necessary treatment. In certain cases the statutory services cannot assess what is happening nor communicate effectively what they are doing. For example, they do not know that certain ethnic minorities are not used to a welfare state or the particular education system and practices in Britain. Without understanding the changes experienced by migrant parents and the traditional attitudes to these provisions brought from the homeland, the services do not know how to, and cannot effectively, explain the use and workings of their personnel and provisions. The mutual misunderstandings which result cause uncertainty and frustration on both sides.

There are straightforward explanations of the fact that few South Asian parents attend parents' meetings; or that the majority of English teachers are against their pupils attending supplementary school to learn their mother tongue; and there are good reasons why an unusually high percentage of West African children are fostered, and why the psychiatric services are underused by South Asians in Britain. Some of these explanations are no different from those pertaining to sections of the indigenous population; others are already known and understood but cannot be acted upon because of very real constraints on resources and trained manpower.

This volume argues that the overall situation can be eased by improving communication and co-operation between researchers and practitioners in the field. It limits itself to presenting information new to many practitioners; and to suggesting an approach based on mutual consultation. It does not argue for more talk and less activity, but for the incorporation of experience gained from existing projects into the debate. At present many field-workers are frustrated by detached, 'ivory-tower' academics, and those academics who have been drawn into issues 'of the real world' are no less frustrated by what they see. The constraints against their dialogue and joint activity are very real and any improvement of existing channels for communication and collaboration will pay important dividends.

Alternative perspectives

The reading material available to help teachers, social workers and other practitioners understand their position in relation to the minorities with whom they work shows the inadequacies of the dialogue between researchers and professionals of the statutory services. There are few books written for social workers or teachers, for example, which raise the need for a reassessment and reorganisation of professional assumptions and practices. While introducing details of the background of the various (but often only 'coloured') minorities they tend to reinforce the notion of minorities as 'problems' in need of special help from the caring and educational agencies. Few are able to express the dynamics of day-to-day life in Britain or to illuminate the strengths of minority group organisation – either for members of minorities or for the society as a whole. Nor is there available any description of what the social workers or teachers actually do, or of how they perceive their various tasks and are reacting to the difficulties encountered in relation to minority group clients or pupils. With these deficiencies, it is not surprising that there are few training programmes or training materials which have been expressly developed to help the practitioner adjust to the multicultural work setting.

Similarly many works on ethnic minorities in Britain tend to emphasise the traditional cultural 'backgrounds' and to ignore what is happening here and now in Britain. They tend to study minorities as though they were living apart when even the most isolated minority group is in contact with and is influenced by the wider society. These studies reflect our preoccupation with 'their' side of the ethnic relations equation; the indigenous population and institutions receive minimal attention. Nevertheless, a mutual readjustment is in progress. Both members of minority groups and workers in statutory institutions are constrained by the structures within which they work and live, and by their past experiences. Both are also facing changes in the population and the environment around them. It is the common experience of the relationship between ethnic minorities and the statutory services which has received very little attention.

This volume is a tentative exploration into this relationship. It explores the types of stress and systems of support experienced within the minorities as a result of migration, the settlement process, growing up a member of a 'second generation'; the types of misunderstandings that emerge between minority and majority; and the ways in which practitioners in the statutory services are prepared for and coping with this situation. This approach gives us some insight into the indigenous population and its institutions because the dominant values in British society are necessarily reflected in the attitudes and responses of teachers, social workers and others to minority groups. Yet all the contributors to this volume are aware that further study into the culture and institutions of British society is essential if we are to take adequate account of many of the crucial determinants of ethnic relations. And all of us are keenly aware that the need remains to come to grips with many of the practical issues which could not be tackled in the volume. The papers in this volume provide a starting point for these further enquiries, but no assessment of the practical and policy issues can be done without the full involvement of practitioners and administrators.

Each of these papers focuses on certain aspects of an ethnic minority or of the statutory services. Each paper can be read in its own right, but the introduction and the links placed between each chapter allow the volume also to be read as an integrated whole.

Introducing a framework

The framework to be erected in this section is a simple construction on which the topics of the different papers can be placed in a variety of combinations. It suggests concepts as tools to facilitate this, and points to the foci of different chapters which are elements of the overall construction. Finally it argues that the construction needs to be placed in its historical and geographical context and related to the local economic and political setting. The framework is presented as a guide to the reader to facilitate the connection of themes but also to use as a basis for further elaboration and enquiry beyond the scope of the book.

The *framework* encompasses our society and both majority and minorities within it. The majority British culture and the institutions of the society which are part of it are affected by, amongst many other things, the nature of the various ethnic minorities. While distinctive in certain important ways, the minorities are in other important respects integral parts of the society as a whole. Although many people stress the gulf between majority and minority cultures, and debate whether its cause be externally imposed (by discrimination and racism) or internally desired (by cultural preference), in day-to-day life each affects the other to some degree. There is participation in joint activities, as in the workplace. People do meet, however briefly, in the street, at the clinic and in local shops. And all members of the society are subject to the same political and economic troubles. They have access to the same media coverage, education and medical services, etc. – although they may of course interpret these in very different ways.

While this volume focuses more specifically on the *relationship* between members of ethnic minorities and the statutory services it needs to emphasise that each is part of the single arena of British society. Uneven distribution of power and resources combine with linguistic and cultural differences to hinder direct communication and equal opportunity to participate fully in the society. Whether they choose to do so when there is the opportunity is a question of attitudes, preferences and prejudices, on both sides of the question.

We are looking here (in some cases all too superficially) at the different systems and structures within the ethnic minorities and the majority institutions. We are concentrating on certain individuals, or categories of people, who are trained by and restrained within these structures. Through socialisation into a particular culture and then (in the case of practitioners) into a particular profession, the individuals acquire attitudes and skills which both help and hinder them in interaction between themselves and with 'outsiders'. In the volume we are shown members of different minorities who are brought up in one system and have contact with another system; and we also look at individuals working in institutions of the wider society who interact with members of minorities. Papers on the minorities cover aspects of their whole system (as our knowledge is particularly deficient in this area) and ask what are the difficulties encountered, and what are the mechanisms which support the conservation of that which is known and valued. Papers looking at workers of the statutory services ask more specifically about their relationships with, and perception of, minority group members; they discuss which things are proving difficult and stressful to them, and what aspects of minority culture and organisation could be used to facilitate their work.

Support and stress

This relationship is summarised by a simple construct of opposing forces in social life: the processes of *support* and *stress*. The simplicity of this construct allows us to explore the various meanings of these processes and the many levels on which they operate, and it ensures a dynamic and realistic approach to the complexities and ambiguities of social life.

In ordinary language, the term *support* conjures up notions of strength and help. Things and people or circumstances and experiences which are 'supportive' are either physical (material and human) resources or provide psychological reassurance. *Stress*, on the other hand, implies feelings and processes suggested by terms such as tension, uncertainty, confusion, isolation and experiences of people or groups.

The two types of support illustrated in the papers of this volume are those based on personal ties such as friends, family and kin and those based on more formal, impersonal connections such as the social or medical services. Many first generation migrants come from societies where the statutory systems of support are minimal whereas many English practitioners are from a society where the more personal forms of support have decreased in importance. Many migrants are not keen to accept or able fully to use 'outside' forms of support. Many practitioners, equally constrained by their own culture and experience, are not able to understand or accept the significance of these alternative systems for those who participate in them.

The main types of stress for ethnic minorities in Britain are those arising from the nature of the migration process and the settlement process, including culture contact and discrimination, etc., and from the repercussions of cultural and/or 'racial' minority status in this particular society. While the most normal life is 'stressful', extra stresses arise in these cases from forces external to the minority itself. They are not, however, exclusive to the minorities; many are also shared by the indigenous population in the same socio-economic situation. Similarly many of the systems of support available to members of minorities are not solely the product of the internal workings of the minority culture or the type of migration process. While members of minorities have access to distinctive forms of support unavailable to the indigenous population (for example, financial and close emotional support from kin) many can at the same time utilise the institutions of British society. The crucial questions are: which are used and when? Where do people turn in times of stress? To friends, family, kin or statutory agencies? Do people use several supportive systems at a time or go from one to the other until the situation is solved or eased? What is known about the statutory services and whether people choose to use them, depends on alternative personal sources of support and the perception of the statutory services provided. How accessible, relevant and effective are the alternatives believed to be?

Levels and meanings

Both support and stress can be discussed at several levels of social life. First, there is the support and stress of states of mind. This level includes questions of identity, self-image, world-view and value systems. At this level we could argue, for example, that a coherent world-view will, despite new experiences and internal conflict, structure events and ensure a continuity of meaning. A firmly held value system can be supportive in that it allows a degree of certainty and predictability in daily life. But if constant reinterpretations of experiences are necessary, or if there is a major threat to basic assumptions, some fundamental adaptation is demanded and the challenge to the system may prove profoundly disruptive. For example, the experience of migration and the period of adolescence involve a re-evaluation of self and questioning of allegiances. If the stresses experienced are contained and complete disruption is not faced then such conflicts provide learning for the future.

The second and third levels are those of interaction between individuals, and between individuals and collectivities or groups. At the level of individual interaction close, dependent attachments with parents, siblings, spouse, child and/or friends and relatives provide emotional involvement and companionship. Loss of a loved one through death or physical separation involves in one sense a loss of self and the need to reconstruct the meaning of life. Migration involves the loss of previously supportive relationships in a time of particular need, but it is difficult to establish new relationships of any depth in a strange society. When, at the third level, supportive family and kin systems or groupings of friends or workmates are dislocated or disrupted a reallocation of emotional, social, and material resources is involved.

Thus, the concepts support and stress cover a wide variety of processes, the former tending to cohesion, stability and continuity, the latter to disruption, change and disorder. These terms have multiple meanings. However defined, it is clear that all social life involves elements of both support and stress and neither is *a priori* good or bad. It is normal that the existing balance of tensions and strengths, stability and instability in the social life of an individual, a family or a community should be disrupted, re-assessed and reformulated over time.

Support and stress are context and situation specific. A process that is supportive or stressful in one setting may prove the opposite in another, where other factors change its significance. For example, the back-up supportive systems which make the arranged marriage system or the observance of *purdah* logical and workable in the homeland, do not exist or cannot function fully in a European urban setting. Village Pakistani women are in many respects in stricter seclusion in Britain and West African wives under greater marital pressure living in the more 'liberated' West than they would be in a traditional setting.

The same situation, whether of support or stress, may also be perceived by different participants in a variety of ways. For example, the village kin network, which has been re-established in Britain among some of the larger and more traditional of the Pakistani and Indian populations, provides support to the new arrival in the form of housing, finding work and emotional and financial backing. To the 'outsider' English neighbour in the same area the apparent segregation of the population is perceived as a deliberate statement of not wanting to mix or adapt. Not trying to integrate is taken as a sign of unfriendliness ('sticking to themselves') and potential trouble in the future ('it'll get like South Africa'). Many of these villagers, however, do not have the opportunity to learn English or other social skills necessary for more than superficial communication.

This example also illustrates that the same situation can create elements of support and stress at one and the same time. The village-kin network and the joint family system are both systems that are highly valued by South Asian families in Britain. Their importance in softening the various stresses of arriving and settling in Britain speak warmly of the support and warmth of their family system. But both systems are none the less felt by some members in some situations to be restrictive and oppressive, limiting opportunities and individual freedom.

Fixing the foundations

We must now look to the foundations of our construction. It was necessary to establish a framework in order to focus upon one specific relationship within it. But there is no way that either framework or relationship can be detached from the fundamental economic, historical and political processes which are not only the underlying determinants of our society, but also of its connection with the countries of emigration. Although this volume cannot tackle these fundamental variables, it is important to point to several crucial aspects, because most of the papers in the volume are discussing present-day situations and concentrating on social rather than economic and political factors.

Historically we are now at a relatively early stage in the settlement of large ethnic minorities in our society. The majority of people belonging to ethnic minorities who are the subject of this volume, both migrants and their British-born children, have been in Britain for under thirty years. The difference of the immigration of the 1950s and 1960s, was in the greater percentage of migrants with a greater cultural difference and/or distinctive colour/physical features and their greater number in comparison to earlier influxes (for example, of Jews or Poles). Although, like the previous immigrations, the later migrants arrived at a time when the indigenous population expected an essentially one-way process of 'integrating' into their values and life-styles, they are now living at a time when such assumptions are being re-assessed. Similarly many professionals of the statutory service not only grew up in a period typified by 'the melting-pot' philosophy, but were trained before the process of questioning within the professions had begun. Although the notion of a pluralist society is gaining ground in certain sections of the indigenous society and among a small percentage of professionals it is not the prevailing ethos in Britain. This is the case despite the increasing evidence, of which this volume forms a part, of the likely persistence and re-formulation of minority cultures in our society.

This volume illustrates the immense diversity within the various minorities and the considerable and significant changes taking place within them. But it points also to the dynamics of the situation. The minorities' relationship with both this society and that of their home-lands may both accelerate and slow down the process of change. And it is not inevitable that change will signify acceptance and adoption of that which is known and valued by the British. In subsequent gener-ations there may be less need for certain provisions established to help first-generation migrants but there may still be crucial forms of provision needed by the second generation. They have not been subject to the difficulties experienced by the migrant. But they face the special ambiguities of membership in a family of an ethnic minor-ity and living in a society in which prejudice and discrimination are still common reactions to cultural or phenotypical difference. It is clear that while culturally sensitive practitioners and services will benefit certain sections and sub-cultures of the indigenous popu-lations as much as members of the minorities, there will be no major change in the situation without certain fundamental political, economic and ideological changes.

The participation of members of ethnic minorities is of crucial importance to the dialogue proposed by this volume. In recent years there has been a gradual increase in the number of social workers, community workers, teachers, etc. from ethnic minorities back-grounds, although the very small numbers of West Indian teachers in Britain is frequently cited as an area of great concern. There are also a small number of researchers from the various minorities studying their own populations, but they are not yet studying British 'ethnics' or the institutions of British society. Despite the participation of people from different minorities, in all professions there remains the question of communication between the minorities and the wider society, and the need to avoid getting an unrepresentative or élite viewpoint. This, like so many other comments in this volume, is a danger in the majority society as a whole. The question remains: which mechanisms will most effectively put forward the minority viewpoints and yet facilitate the direct participation of ordinary people in spheres of influence in the wider society?

This question reminds us that the political perspective must be closely related to the historical considerations. The changes that are at present under way are not solely the result of the passage of time and the gradual settlement and re-orientation of minorities. Many migrants came with a 'target' intending to return and so making every effort to save money, and minimise any form of trouble or 'stick'. They came when there was a demand for their labour and little pre-occupation in this country with what has subsequently become known as the 'race relations and immigration debate'. This has developed into a highly sensitive and politicised topic at a time of economic crisis and high unemployment. Just as the minorities were settling in to and participating more fully in the society, the country has had to face a period of economic difficulty and adjust to its loss of significance on the international scene.

These factors it can be argued have contributed to an increase in the resentment felt toward previously 'subject' people of the British Empire. Whatever the contributing factors, it is clear that the rise of right-wing movements and the emotional use of the 'race' issue by the media and by certain prominent politicians, hinders the trend towards the minorities' participation in and identification with this country. The insecurity generated by the politicisation of these issues and by the increase in violent verbal and physical attacks has caused many families to re-assess their position and the future of their children in this country. It alters the patterns and definitions of support and stress used and experienced by them and by those members of British society working for their well-being and so for the collective well-being of our society.

1

This paper focuses on the supportive mechanisms used by Cypriots in their migration to Britain. Personalised systems of support – of family, kin and patronage – are typical of the chain migration process, and are a notable feature of many other mass migrations to Britain. An unusual aspect of this case is the degree of involvement in the process by the government of the country of emigration. This additional institutionalised system of support is shown here to have reinforced existing supportive systems of the traditional culture.

We are reminded as we read this paper that many characteristics associated with black and brown minorities in Britain are also features of those white minorities who, similarly, have originated from rural areas of the homeland and settled in Britain in large numbers in a relatively short period of time.

Family, Kinship and Patronage

The Cypriot migration to Britain

Robin Oakley

This paper is concerned principally to examine the family composition of post-war Cypriot migrants to Britain, and to discuss the role of kinship and other social ties in the process of migration. It begins by outlining the more general features of Cypriot migration and describing briefly the traditional culture and society of Cyprus from which the migrants derive. The sections that follow outline the role of family, kinship and patronage ties in the migration. Finally, in a concluding section, the influence of government regulation of the migration on social organisation is considered.

The data presented are drawn from a broader study of Cypriot migration and settlement in Britain,[1] based largely on official statistical and other published sources, but including also information obtained through participant observation among Cypriots in London and in Cyprus during 1965–7. For the purpose of that study, and this paper, the post-war migration of Cypriots to Britain is considered as a movement which was in effect completed by 1966. This is partly because by that year the number of migrants (and especially labour migrants) had dwindled to the level almost of its post-war beginnings, and partly because it was convenient to take the British population census carried out that year as a principal source of data on Cypriot settlement in Britain. The migration of Cypriots to Britain has in fact continued since that time, but at very low levels, with the one exception of the year 1974–5. Following renewed inter-ethnic conflict on the island that year, several thousands of Cypriots entered Britain on a short-stay basis as unofficial 'refugees' from the fighting and territorial displacement.[2] The circumstances of their departure from Cyprus were therefore very different from those of their predecessors. For this reason, therefore, it must be emphasised that the data refer only to the large-scale migration which took place during the first two post-war decades. The family and kinship patterns of these more recent immigrants, and of present-day Cypriots in Britain, would need to be the subject of separate study.[3]

The use of the term 'Cypriot' requires comment. According to religion and national identification, Cypriots differentiate themselves into two ethnic categories, 'Greek' and 'Turkish', each with its own educational system. There has been little consciousness of being collectively 'Cypriot' as a cultural or national identity. In terms of other social and economic characteristics, however, and especially during the colonial period, the two groups have shown broad similarities. Among the migrants to Britain, about four-fifths are Greek in ethnic terms, and about one-fifth Turkish – a similar ratio, in fact, to that among the population of Cyprus as a whole. In this paper the term Cypriot is used to refer to both groups. In the general section on migration, and where official documents and statistics are used, this is fully appropriate. However, in the main parts of the paper where kinship structure and patronage are discussed, the data refer overtly to Greek Cypriot migrants only. Differences between the Greek and Turkish migrants in these respects are undoubtedly more apparent than real, but they exist, and their extent and character would have to be established by further research.[4]

The migration

The migration of Cypriots to Britain may be seen as part of the wider movement of immigration from the New Commonwealth countries to Britain that has occurred during the post-war period. The roots of the migration must therefore be seen in the island's colonial past.

Although Cyprus only acquired the formal status of a British Colony in 1925 the history of Britain's colonial relationship with the island dates back to 1878 when Cyprus, at that time part of the decaying Ottoman Empire, was made a British Protectorate. From then right up to present, Britain's interest in the island has been essentially strategic and not economic. Concern with the circumstances of the Cypriots themselves has therefore been limited to two areas: the need to maintain political stability internally, and the provision of the minimum economic infrastructure sufficient to meet the requirements of a military presence.

The post-war emigration from the island must be understood in the context of the extension of Cypriot horizons beginning with the war-time experiences, and a raising of economic expectations linked to the massive, although in scope limited, economic investment undertaken by the government and military authorities during the 1950s. The inability of this to lead to any self-sustaining economic expansion, combined with the political instability and eventual British Government withdrawal on Independence in 1960, precipitated a mass movement of emigrants seeking to take advantage of employment opportunities in Britain in the late 1950s and early 1960s. The continued British military presence on the island is still a major source of employment locally. But economic and renewed political pressures towards emigration have persisted and continuing movement to Britain has been curbed only because of Britain's stringent control first of 'Commonwealth', and now 'non-patrial' immigration.

Although the vast majority of Cypriot migrants to Britain travelled during the post-war period, it is important to note that the origins of the movement are pre-war. Indeed, by the outbreak of the Second World War in 1939 it was officially estimated that there were already some 8000 Cypriots settled in London. In many ways this original nucleus provided a foundation on which the large-scale post-war settlement could grow. After the war, in the period up to 1966, a further 75,000 Cypriots left their island as emigrants to Britain. At first the movement picked up slowly, but it accelerated during the 1950s, to reach a peak of over 12,000 emigrants in both 1960 and 1961. Thereafter the flow of immigrants declined sharply in response to the tightening of the labour market in Britain and the imposition of increasingly severe British immigration controls. By 1966 the number of migrants leaving Cyprus for Britain annually had fallen below 2000 and the total admitted to Britain for employment (rather than as dependants, etc.) had been reduced to a mere 80 persons.

None the less, the overall size of Cypriot settlement in Britain had by this time reached a total of approximately 100,000 persons (including children born in Britain). Three-quarters of these were resident within Greater London, especially in the boroughs stretching north from the central area. Among Greek Cypriots particularly, a flourishing community had grown up, building on small pre-war beginnings

in the restaurant trade and diversifying into a variety of craft businesses as well as into a range of services. This meant that in terms of
employment and consumer requirements the community was to a
high degree self-sufficient in providing for its needs.[5] This economic
organisation was complemented by a network of churches and political associations and also by numerous less formal associations, linked
mainly with particular villages in Cyprus or with leisure activities
such as sports. Among Turkish Cypriots the degree of organisation at
community level has been far less than this, but overall it could be
said that Cypriot immigrants constructed a world within which,
given certain necessary adaptations, they have been able (in the first
generation at least) to maintain a sense of ethnic solidarity and to
preserve, broadly speaking, their traditional culture and life-style.

The cultural background

Cyprus is a small island in the Eastern·Mediterranean with a mixed
agricultural economy which has traditionally been organised on the
basis of individual peasant land-holdings, often highly fragmented.
Industrialisation has been limited and has taken place only slowly.
Urbanisation has proceeded to some degree, but the island towns
have developed primarily as local administrative and market centres,
and at the 1960 census only Nicosia (the capital) had a population of
the order of 100,000 inhabitants. Traditional patterns of culture and
social organisation have thus continued relatively unchanged
throughout the Colonial period.

   The social world from which the great majority of migrants have
come, whether directly or indirectly via a period of employment in
one of the regional towns on the island, has been that of the village,
and above all that of the family group.[6] Cyprus is an island of some
600 villages; and with a total population of less than 600,000 at the
1960 census, the average village size is clearly small. The Cypriot
village may be described typically as a fairly compact community of
small autonomous family groups, closely interconnected by numerous ties of marriage and descent. By 'family' is meant here the nuclear
unit of married parents and their children, with perhaps elderly or
widowed grandparents living in the household as well. Kinship is
reckoned bilaterally, though on marriage residence would normally
be taken up in the husband's village rather than that of the wife.

But despite the ubiquity and undoubted importance of these wider ties of kinship, each individual family aims to be a sovereign and self-reliant unit. Family loyalty is the paramount virtue. This involves, on the one hand, the obligation to put immediate family first, and kin generally before others. On the other, in the competitive and critical atmosphere of village life, it entails the obligation always to maintain and promote the honour and reputation of the family, by discharging one's roles and responsibilities in a manner as near as possible to that prescribed by the gender-differentiated cultural ideals. As head of the family and its representative in all public matters, particular responsibility in this respect falls upon the husband/father, but it is a responsibility that is shared by each other individual as a member of the family as a whole. Within traditional Cypriot society, therefore, the family is the basic, indeed the sole, solidary group: each family farms its own land, runs its household, travels, celebrates and generally faces the world as a single unit.

Outside the family, loyalties are always secondary and uncertain, even though ties of near kin (especially married siblings) are close and of great importance. They are important above all in modern conditions where economic and educational opportunities often require reliable relationships to be established by families outside their own village. In these circumstances, ties between more distant kin may be cemented, or new relationships created, by the construction of 'pseudo-kinship' in the institution of 'godparenthood' or 'wedding-sponsorship' (*koumbaria*). In this way more contractual relationships – especially those of 'patronage' – may be set up, overlapping or complementing those of kinship proper, so as to provide for needs which cannot be adequately met within the kinship system as such.

In the light of this outline of Cypriot cultural background it is not surprising to find the post-war migration to be strongly characterised by family and kinship patterning. This is examined in the following two sections.

The family composition of the migration

The primary social unit in relation to which Cypriot migration must be understood is that of the nuclear family, whether the migrant is a member of a family unit or a single individual as yet unmarried. The act of migration is integrally bound up with the characteristic structure and developmental cycle of the Cypriot family. The official migration statistics of Cyprus[7] show that over the major period of migration, from 1955–66, the sex ratio among migrants was relatively balanced, with males predominating in a ratio of approximately 110 to every 100 females. The age distribution showed a marked concentration in the younger age groups, with more than half of the migrants aged between fifteen and thirty-four years (see Table 1.1). Concentration in the range fifteen and twenty-four years was particularly marked among males and it is the relatively greater population of men than women in this young adult age group that largely accounts for the overall disparity between the sexes. This age and sex distribution suggests that a combination of family and individual migration took place, with marked predisposition for migration to have occurred at certain stages of the family development cycle. Moreover, it can be estimated that around 60 per cent of Cypriot women and around 45 per cent of men migrants were already married before they left the island.[8]

TABLE 1.1   *Age and sex of Cypriot migrants, 1955–66 (percentages)*

	Male	Female	Total
0–4	8.8	9.3	9.1
5–14	15.7	16.8	16.3
15–24	35.4	31.0	33.2
25–34	18.0	18.3	18.1
35–44	10.4	10.3	10.4
45–54	6.4	7.6	7.0
55–64	3.8	4.8	4.3
65+	1.5	1.7	1.6
Total	100.0	100.0	100.0
N	37,448	34,396	71,844

SOURCE   Republic of Cyprus, Ministry of Finance, *Vital and Migration Statistics* and *Demographic Reports* (Nicosia, annual).

The typical family emigrating from Cyprus has had one, two or perhaps three children, most commonly of primary or pre-school age.[9] In the earlier and peak periods of the migration, pre-school predominated over older children, although in the later period of controlled immigration to Britain during which 'dependants' of earlier settlers predominated, the five- to nine-year-old category was the largest (see Table 1.2). Thus, while there has clearly been much variation in the size and character of families there has been a predominance of small families with young children, in contrast to the traditionally larger families on the island.

TABLE 1.2   *Age of children among Cypriot migrants, 1955–66 (percentages)*

	1955–61	*1962–6*
0–4	39.0	30.6
5–9	33.9	40.1
10–14	27.1	29.3
All children	100.0	100.0
N	12,115	5,907

SOURCE   Republic of Cyprus, Ministry of Finance, *Vital and Migration Statistics* and *Demographic Reports* (Nicosia, annual).

Most husbands journeyed ahead, the wife and children following later. In this way the husband could explore possibilities, establish himself in a job, and then save up for fares and suitable housing so that he could bring the rest of his family over to join him. This is illustrated by the following instance.

Mr H. arrived in Britain in 1956. He had married two years earlier and had a baby son. His village was close to the district town of Larnaca where he had been able to get intermittent labouring work, mainly in the construction industry. His elder brother, who had left for Britain several years earlier, urged him to join him; so having saved enough for his own and part of his wife's passage, he left the island to find a job in London, leaving his wife and child with her parents in the neighbouring village. His brother's plan for him to obtain work in a tailoring business did not work out, but he soon found work instead in the kitchen of a major West End hotel. Part of his wage he sent back to help support his wife and child at home, while from the rest he gradually saved up the extra money needed for his wife's passage to London. Eventually, about five months after his departure he was able to send for her and the baby to join him in the single room he had rented above a shop in Camden Town.

In the majority of cases the period apart was a matter of months, or perhaps a year, but sometimes the husband did not send for his family for several years. Table 1.3, drawn from a study of Cypriot immigration in London in 1957–8, indicates the variation among emigrant families in length of separation between couples. These figures do not of course measure how far the family unit has remained a viable social entity during this period, through visiting, remittances and the support of wider kin. Nor does it give any indication of the number of marriages which may have been permanently broken consequent upon the husband's emigration.

TABLE 1.3   *Time disparity of arrival of married couples among Cypriot immigrants in Britain, 1957–8 (percentages)*

	Total	1–12 months	1–2 years	2–5 years	5–10 years
Wife before husband ·	3	3	–	–	–
Husband/wife together	40	–	–	–	–
Husband before wife	57	20	17	13	7
Total	100	23	17	13	7
N	150				

SOURCE   V. Nearchou, 'The Assimilation of Cypriot Immigrants in London', MA thesis (University of Nottingham, 1960) p. 48. Data obtained from the Government of Cyprus' London Office, for Cypriot families resident in London in 1957–8.

Single persons, however, as we have already seen, constituted the other half of adult Cypriots migrating to Britain. The neat dichotomy of 'single' versus 'married' is, however, dangerous. In traditional Cypriot society the term 'single' person has meaning only in terms of the phase of the traditional life-cycle when a young person ceases to be dependent on parents but has yet to acquire the responsibilities assumed on marriage. Migration as such may express this independence; it may also be a means of improving marriage prospects in social and economic terms, or even of seeking a marriage partner direct, i.e. free from the traditional limitation of the parentally arranged match.

These considerations do not apply equally for both boys and girls. For boys, there is a cultural expectation that they should pass through a phase of relative independence between childhood and the attainment of full adult status in marriage. This is the period of emergent manhood, summed up in the traditional cultural ideals of the *pallikari* – courage, honour, freedom, and thus a living proof of a boy's worthiness to assume the adult role. Traditionally, this phase often involved a young man leaving home and seeking honour by travelling 'abroad' (metaphorically, if not literally). Such cultural expectations still prove of some importance in the motivation of young Cypriot men emigrating overseas. Nevertheless, marriage remains the eventual goal, although for men the median age in modern Cyprus is some five years later than for women. Marriage prospects, and the shared responsibility for those of one's siblings, especially the dowries of sisters, are therefore essential concerns of young men. Emigration to Britain represents a further opportunity to advance their own and their families' interests mainly through the prospects of better marriages. This is in contrast to the already married migrants for whom migration has commonly represented the obligation to meet responsibilities already contracted (for example, providing economically for their families when jobs are unavailable at home).

For single girls the cultural ideals prescribe a pattern of conduct which renders their migration independent of families less expected and less readily approved. This is reflected in the fact that the unmarried are a smaller proportion among women than among men. In part this may be attributed to the lower age of marriage as such, but this differential alone accounts for only about half the discrepancy. The motivation of women is different, and cultural attitudes prescribe that no unmarried girl should emigrate without her parents, unless she goes to join close kin, or to marry immediately on arrival. Girls are expected to have a relatively passive and brief period before an offer of marriage. During this time the principal tasks, besides her family's preparation of the dowry, is to evince the 'shame' appropriate to her sex (the counterpart of male 'honour') through the modesty of her manner and the seclusion or protective supervision of her person. Where paid employment is available a girl could contribute directly to her marriage prospects through earning towards her dowry, although this is opposed to the cultural expectation of modesty and seclusion appropriate to her sex. But the availability in Britain of emigré kin, and of appropriately supervised workplaces (which enable some relaxation of the strict traditional ideals), has enabled the emigration of unmarried girls without the loss of family honour.

Marriage is, however, often the immediate prospect for Cypriot girls emigrating to Britain. Changing attitudes in Cyprus may also have facilitated such migration, and for village-born girls it has often been rendered the more necessary as a route to marriage by the acute shortage of eligible young men in some areas due to levels of intra-island as well as overseas migration.

Although the great majority of migrants have been single people or units of parents with young children, a small proportion of migrants have been elderly persons (as shown in Table 1.1). Approximately 6 per cent of migrants were aged fifty-five or over, and therefore unlikely to be supporting themselves directly through employment. This points to the tendency for established migrants to bring over their elderly parents, especially when no brother or sister is left in Cyprus to support them, or if the parent is a widowed person, particularly a widowed mother. That the latter is more common is evident from the higher proportion of women in the senior age categories in the migration statistics. This obligation to support elderly parents brings with it the advantage of having a grandmother in the migrant home to help care for the children. However, the close proximity of the two senior generations, when the three-generation family is under a single roof, may also bring tensions that were absent in the more outdoor and spatially separated life-style of the Cyprus village.

Kinship in the migration process

Cypriot migration may be seen, then, as a process wherein families dissolve, are re-created, or move as existing units with or without some temporary separation, the actual patterns varying according to circumstances. But although families and individuals are for the most part expected to act freely and autonomously in this respect, they do so commonly in the context of ties and potential obligation to wider kin, on whom they draw support in the process of migration. This may be prescribed, as in the case of emigration of unmarried girls, or may merely be an opportunity to be used where available and which should be granted whenever it is sought. As children grow up and are less dependent on their parents, so they often turn to adult siblings for aid and support, as well as uncles, aunts and cousins.

The extent to which this has been the case can be illustrated by a survey among Commonwealth immigrants in Britain conducted in 1961. This indicated that two-thirds of Cypriot immigrants had one or more siblings living here, and almost half had at least two other siblings in Britain.[10] As might be expected, brothers were more common than sisters, three-fifths having brothers in Britain and rather less than two-fifths sisters. However, as many who had brothers in Britain also had brothers in Cyprus, indicating that it is unusual for all the siblings of a family to leave by emigrating overseas.

This survey did not enquire also into the presence of wider kin, such as cousins, in-laws and uncles and aunts who may also play important roles in respect of migration and settlement. This was evident from personal enquiry among Cypriots both in London (for example, the instances cited) and in Cyprus where it was exceedingly rare to find a person who could not quote some relative of his acquaintance who was already living in Britain. Indeed, not to have such a contact required explanation.

What exactly is the significance of these wider ties of kinship in the process of migration from Cyprus to Britain? There are various degrees and kinds of assistance that may be given by kinsmen and others in the process of migration. Perhaps the first important role of kinsmen in the migration process lies simply in the provision of information. Letters and visits both ways are the important means of communication between the home country and the settlement overseas. Letters provide for a continuous and very rapid exchange of information between settlers and their kin at home. They give news of the health and welfare of the family and relatives, and details of arrangements of important matters, such as property transactions or visits. A single letter may be quite widely circulated and so can provide information for a large number of people. Further information can be obtained from the press. Cypriots are traditionally avid readers of newspapers, and in recent times Cyprus dailies have carried weekly supplements with 'News of Cypriots in Britain'.

Visiting is a regular feature of communication between the two communities, and passenger statistics testify to its scale. The number of Cypriot visitors to Cyprus from Britain averaged about 4000 a year during the 1960s up to 1966, the figure reaching approximately 9000 in the last of the years.[11] This latter figure approaches one tenth of the total estimated Cypriot population in Britain. Almost all of these Cypriots returning to Cyprus on temporary visits gave 'holidays' as the purpose for their visit, and were visiting relatives on the island. Figures for visitors moving in the reverse direction, from Cyprus to Britain, show a similar average rate of visiting of around 4000 per year. Most of these Cypriots, too, were visiting relatives, only this time it would be the immigrants who played host. A small proportion of visitors between the two countries travel for other reasons, such as business purposes or for medical treatment. Those visiting relatives may also be considering the possibility of a permanent move, as outward or return migrants. A visit of this kind is an opportunity for them to assess the prospects:

Mr L., a small shopkeeper in north London, had a good friend (in fact, a second cousin) in Cyprus whom he encouraged to visit Britain to see what life here might offer him.[12] *Mr L. already stood as* koumbaros *(wedding sponsor) to him. The friend came over early in summer and stayed for some months with relatives, during which time Mr L. showed him all round London and other parts of Britain. They had a marvellous time, but the friend did not decide to settle and returned to Cyprus. However, he was extremely thankful to Mr L. for all that he had done on his behalf, and Mr L.'s family now regularly receive huge parcels of fresh Cyprus produce from him. Mr L. himself has not been back to Cyprus for several years because of the expense of taking his whole family along, though also because of the difficulty of leaving his work. His wife's unmarried sister, however, has recently been back for several months staying with her married brother in his house in the town. His two elder children were currently spending the summer in Cyprus, chiefly with their grandparents in the parents' own village, though in part also with other relatives in the district town.*

The provision of finance for the journey, and of other resources in kind such as housing, are also important needs of the migrant which are frequently met by kinsmen. To travel abroad cheaply and exploratorily as a young man is one thing, but to move with an already formed family is another. This is one of the main reasons why a father will often journey ahead, and if he cannot raise the necessary money otherwise, will save up from his wages to bring over the rest of the family later. The direct assistance of kin may be called upon at both ends of the migration: relatives in Cyprus to provide housing and general support for family members left behind (and to look after any other interests such as village land), and relatives in Britain to provide housing, assistance with finding employment, and where necessary to provide personal guarantees of support (required for the issue of emigration permits in Cyprus up to 1969 – see below). Many of those roles of kinsmen in the migration process were illustrated in the example of Mr H. (above). The following instance of how a successful migrant began his career illustrates further the typical importance of the kinship context within which migration takes place:

Mr N. came to Britain in 1950 when he was 20 years old, and he now runs a shoe-mending business in a busy area of north London. He was one of seven children, and one of his elder brothers had been in England since before the war. His only sister, too, was already in London by 1950. After he left school at the age of fourteen towards the end of the war, he had for some time a good job in the building trade, but by the end of the decade it had become difficult to find regular work outside his village. He therefore arranged with this brother in London, who was himself a shoemaker by trade, to take him on temporarily as an assistant in his shop. His brother provided the necessary guarantees for the issue of a passport, and in due course Mr N. arrived in London. He lived with his brother and worked in his shop for the best part of a year, so as to learn the trade and to save up some money. He then took the lease on a shop elsewhere, and set up in business on his own. In 1953, at his parents' suggestion, he returned to Cyprus to marry a girl from his home village, and they returned together soon afterwards. She already had a number of cousins who collectively run one of the most successful Cypriot clothing businesses in London; in addition she had an elder sister who runs a smaller dressmaking factory quite close to where they were living where two other cousins are also employed. On arrival she worked there for a couple of months, but after she had settled down she preferred to remain at home with her husband, doing piece-work on her own machine at her convenience. Nowadays, with their business well established, she helps her husband in the shop, and only uses her machine to meet her own needs and those of her children.

This example is fairly typical of the role of kinsmen in the migration of Cypriots to Britain. A young man, speaking little English, possessing no particular skill and largely ignorant of city life, would have a negligible chance of success unless he could rely on someone to provide both security and some framework for his own personal adjustment in the initial period of settlement. The requirement of an 'affidavit of support' prior to the issue of a passport (see below) formalised a link between migrant and established resident which would have been desirable for most migrants anyway. In the example quoted, both the man and his new wife were reliant on their respective siblings at the start of their lives in Britain. In the wife's case, there was the additional factor of adjusting to her new husband (whom at the time she was barely acquainted with). If she had come as a wife of several years standing, she would no doubt have had less need of support from her own relatives.

Outside this immediate circle of first-degree kin, the degree of obligation is not so complete. Assistance can be expected, but some reckoning of mutual advantage is likely to be made, especially where considerable burden or risk is involved. First cousins and in-laws are sometimes very close, but as one moves further away the commitment is weaker, and the more the relationship needs to be buttressed by some kind of unwritten contractual arrangement. Even if a job is given, hard work is expected, and although a room is provided, rent is to be paid. Competitiveness tends to keep such co-operative relationships evenly balanced, or else it destroys them. However, where the kin relationship concerned crosses a generation, such as with uncle and nephew, this reciprocity is not always apparent. Aid might be given regardless, simply because the nephew is the son of one's brother. Even so, whatever the motive, the senior man expects to receive the respect of the junior in return, and thus enhance his own prestige in the eyes of the community.

Patronage in the migration process

This element of deference and prestige in social relationships is the basis of another kind of institutionalised relationship, which is important in the social context of Cypriot migration. This is the relationship of patronage.[13] Just as with kinship, patronage may manifest itself in a number of different forms, and may connote a variety of different roles. Essentially, however, patronage implies an inequality of status, and a flow of favours from the superior partner which cannot be matched by the junior, who in exchange gives recognition to the prestige and influence of his patron. Moreover, it provides a framework within which a man, who has needs which cannot be met within his kinship network, can ask and obtain favours of others without losing his own self-respect, and in accordance with an accepted set of norms as to how this is to be done.

Sometimes, in fact, patronage and kinship relationships overlap, as suggested, for instance, in the preceding section when talking of uncles and nephews. However, where there is no pre-existent kin tie between the two parties involved in a relationship of patronage, a relationship of 'spiritual kinship' (*koumbaria*) may be created.[14] This 'pseudo-kinship' tie is initiated by the dependent party inviting the patron to be among his wedding sponsors (*koumbari*) at his marriage, and then subsequently (or alternatively, initially) to 'baptise' one or more of his children. The tie that is thereby set up between families, and particularly between godparent and godchild, lasts for life and is almost as important as the ties of kinship proper. Ceremonially, it is regarded as a relationship of consanguinity. The privileges and responsibilities which are associated with it are treated with great seriousness, for a well-chosen godfather or marriage sponsor can provide or arrange important favours. He in turn can be assured of much prestige and support in any political pursuits.

A relationship of patronage tends to be established *with* the act of migration rather than being a previous condition for this act. This is because the patron has become so through his successful establishment in Britain. Patrons in Britain are generally those who on settlement began 'at the bottom' and who have gradually built up for themselves a successful business. Having brought over first of all their closest kin, they then recruit from a wider circle of relatives and co-villagers. They may recruit also from the families of friends in Britain, or of employees to whom they stand in a relationship of patronage. As far as the actual migrant and his patron are concerned, however, it is the personal favour of facilitating migration which creates the bond. Over time, therefore, a successful businessman can build up a ramifying structure of patronage which amounts to a considerable personal following. What use he makes of this following is of course another matter; this depends on a variety of factors. None the less, patronage is an important feature of the social organisation of Cypriot life in Britain, and of the migration between the two islands. But its presence in any relationship is not often visible to the casual acquaintance and its workings are subtle: often it is concealed and formalised in the idiom of kinship or its ceremonial counterpart. The following example illustrates clearly how over time an enterprising individual can build up a substantial structure of patronage by arranging for migration.

Mr T. was one of the earliest Cypriot migrants to arrive in Britain, and he now runs a successful restaurant in the West End of London. Like most other early migrants who arrived in the inter-war period, he started off by working in the kitchens of London hotels, but by the 1930s he had worked his way up to the position of banqueting manager at one well-known West End hotel. Shortly before the war he opened his present restaurant, and in the post-war years has expanded it so that he now has a staff of between thirty-five and forty persons, almost all Cypriots. To use his own words: 'When I could help my family I brought over one brother, then a second, then a third; then two sisters, then a cousin, and then another one – then two nephews, and some second cousins and about fifty or more people whom I was asked, from time to time, to help. I am glad to say they all, with almost no exceptions, did exceedingly well. My brothers run two hotels (in a town on the south coast) – small affairs but enough to keep them independent, my nephews have two bigger hotels, a restaurant and a club (in the same town) and some of the others I helped are in their own businesses and doing

*very well thank you!' The first brother Mr T. helped to come over in 1928, when
he could already arrange a job for him through his own position of responsibility,
and other family members followed during the 1930s. However, it was when he
opened a restaurant of his own, and the size of his staff grew, that he was able to
bring over larger numbers of people. All these were personally indebted to him
since under the 'affidavit' system, in operation from 1937 onwards, they were
dependent on Mr T's guarantee of a job and of general security without
which they could not have made the journey. In due course, many have moved on to
other jobs leaving more vacancies to be filled, some setting up restaurants of their
own in which the same process of recruitment along kinship and patronage lines is
repeated.*

Mr T. is one of those Cypriots whose success in business has not
been matched by a desire for influence or by aspiration for political
office within the Cypriot community. His interest is confined to the
running of this one high-class restaurant, and in many ways he stands
outside the Cypriot community properly speaking. In marked contrast is the following example of a man who has been the founder of a
small but flourishing Cypriot community in a large provincial city.

*Mr K. arrived in London shortly before the war in the role of lace-merchant,
being brought over by his brother-in-law who was already established in the
trade. At first he worked in London hotels, but during the war he ran several
businesses of his own, one after the other, landing up in 1954 with a basement café
in his present place of residence. He began with the company of just his own
family, subsequently adding one or two new staff from time to time. But when Mr
K. moved to a larger café, opening a second and then a third business, he brought
over more and more relatives and villagers from Cyprus for work in the kitchens
and as waiters. By the time his three daughters were ready to be married, Mr K.
was in a position to provide his sons-in-law with a café each to run: 'as dowries?'
– 'sort of', he acknowledges with a smile. In the last five to ten years, the growth
of Cypriot enterprise in this town has been rapid, rising from just a few businesses
in the late 1950s to around twenty in 1966. Some are run by those who had
previously experienced Mr K's patronage, while others were started by outsiders.
However, as Mr K. points out, it is today financially much more difficult to start
up on one's own than it was around the war-time, unless, that is, one has the
patronage of some wealthy relative, as do his own sons-in-law. On the whole,
though, he reckons that he now has well over 100 relatives within the city itself and
many more in the district around, his sister, cousins and other relatives owning
restaurants and coffee bars in the neighbouring towns. About half the thousand-
odd Cypriot population of the city derives from either his small mountain village
or from the two other villages close by, while more come from his wife's home*

village further off. In fact, almost all come from this overall region of Cyprus, and have some kind of personal connection, if indirect, with Mr K. In this way, he has built up a large personal following within this Cypriot 'colony'. Now that a formally organised 'community' has been established by the Greeks in the town, with a committee, church, priest and school, Mr K. is naturally the respected and influential President. His wealth, the prestige gained from his beneficent patronage, and his own personal character are the crucial factors behind this success, though he relies increasingly on his sons-in-law for co-operation in running this flourishing Greek community.

This further example needs little comment for it shows again how patronage operates in regard to migration and settlement, and how at the same time it can give rise to an informal pyramid of prestige and influence which can be transformed into a formal structure of authority. Within London, as opposed to outside in the provinces, such self-contained political units are less likely to occur in view of the size of the settlement, its relative heterogeneity, and the greater job opportunities and mobility of its members. None the less, both instances show the importance of patronage in the migration, particularly in the provision of employment prospects and the provision of formal guarantees in this respect when this was officially required. In some cases prospective employers also advanced money to pay for fares, against wages that would be earned on arrival. Such contractual ties may therefore be established and utilised particularly in cases where appropriate kin ties have been unavailable, or in areas of need, such as employment, where kin have been unable to make direct provision.

Governmental involvement in the migration process

The institutionalised patterns of personal relationship in family, kin and patronage constitute the social structure of Cypriot migration at the primary level. They are the means whereby social continuity has been maintained and where there would otherwise be disruption and change. It is important to recognise, however, that the organisation of the migration process also involves secondary level structures of an impersonal nature and with more specific functions. These structures comprise first of all the organisation of travel facilities, and secondly the bureaucratic procedures of departure and admission in the countries concerned.

As the cost and conditions of travel improved in the 1950s, so it came within reach of increasing numbers of Cypriots, and travel agencies sprang up to provide tickets for passages and the full range of financial and other services required by prospective migrants. These agencies, operating mainly from North London but with branches in Cyprus, advertised regularly in the Cyprus press and also in the immigrant weeklies published in London. By 1966 there were at least ten such agencies, though by this time the greatest part of their business was devoted not to migration as such, but to visits to and fro between emigrants and their kin. Travel agencies did not merely facilitate the operation of kinship and patronage ties in the migration process, but offered an alternative source of support when this was not available elsewhere. The participation of the respective governments in the migration process, on the other hand, has been solely regulatory in character, with interventions designed to meet specific purposes and with specific effect. Programmes of migrant recruitment, schemes for formal sponsorship or routine aid, have not been in operation at any time.

Both the Cyprus and British governments, each for part of the period only, imposed controls on the migration, which had the effect of promoting personal sponsorship at the expense of independent movement. The regulation of migration to Britain by the Cypriot government was initiated as early as 1937 because of the Cyprus government's concern over the conditions of Cypriot immigrants in London at the time. Before prospective migrants were issued with appropriate documents for travel overseas, they had to meet three requirements; that they could speak an adequate amount of English: they should be able to deposit the sum of £30, against themselves or their dependants becoming destitute and requiring financial aid; and that they should have a job awaiting them on arrival in Britain, and that a guarantee of support should have been made on their behalf by a relative or friend who was an 'established resident' in Britain. It was the duty of the Liaison Officer at the government's London Office to investigate such offers of support: to enquire into their *bona fides*; and to satisfy himself that there was no unemployment in the trade in question. If the outcome of his investigation was positive, an 'affidavit of support' could then be issued and forwarded to Cyprus.

After the war, the regulation of Cypriot emigration continued along essentially the same lines. In addition, more careful investigation was made into the welfare of families of prospective migrants. From the early 1950s onwards, the Department of Social Welfare Services in

Cyprus[15] enquired into the welfare situation of the families of prospective migrants, and no passport was issued to an applicant until the District Welfare Officer's report had been received and considered. From 1956 onwards, investigations were made only where dependent children were involved. Under the Children's Law, the Welfare Department was enabled 'to object to the issue of a passport to an applicant who intends to leave Cyprus without taking his child or children with him, if it appears that such child or children are likely to become a charge on public funds or to be exposed to moral danger or neglect by reason of lack of care or maintenance'.[16]

The affidavit system, for its part, seems to have worked fairly smoothly, at least up to 1954. Around the mid-1950s, however, it seems that a certain amount of abuse took place. A fee for the issue of an affidavit was introduced but investigations to establish the *bona fides* of guarantors became less thorough, and seem eventually to have ceased altogether. Bribery is alleged to have been common, and agencies offered their services to prospective migrants and employers at fees ranging from £10 to £30, even advertising openly in the Cyprus press. Eventually, in 1959, the 'affidavit system' was discontinued and Cypriots were henceforth able to obtain passports for emigration without meeting any conditions of this kind.

The influence of the Cyprus Government's regulations on the role of family, kinship and patronage in the migration has been two-fold. In the first place, the effect of the Welfare Department's investigators has been to reinforce the family responsibilities of intending migrants. The number of cases investigated by the District Welfare Officer and his Field Officers in the years 1963, 1964 and 1965 were in the region of 700 in each instance. In 1964 objections were made in thirty-five cases, and in 1965 in fifty-four cases (no figure being given for 1963 or any other year). This involved enquiring of the income, dwellings and other property of the family, and of ascertaining what support for the children might be forthcoming from relatives. Where these were found inadequate, and passport issue objected to, the intending migrant was sometimes deterred. Those more determined to migrate were less likely to be put off, and usually made the arrangements required by the Welfare Officer sooner or later. These were often financial in nature, involving the provision of adequate security for the family while the father was away. Sometimes the Department's objections might be met by the father saving from earnings during a few months wage employment or alternatively a relative might be found to give an undertaking to care for the family if they were in difficulty.

Not only did the Department require adequate provision to be made for dependants by the migrant *before* departure: if the husband defaulted once in Britain, then the Department sought to obtain the necessary aid for his dependants from him through the Welfare Officer of the Government's London Office (or, since 1960, High Commission), using the British Courts to obtain a Maintenance Order if necessary. An additional task of the Welfare Department was to reunite children left behind in Cyprus with one or more parents in Britain.[17] The Welfare Department also concerned itself with marital separation due to migration, and was involved in reconciliation of spouses in Britain with those in Cyprus.[18] In these various ways, therefore, the Welfare Department operated services to promote family and marital solidarity in the process of Cypriot migration to Britain, employing conciliation, direct assistance and ultimately legal sanctions in its attempt to support family ties where these appeared to be in danger of breaking or had actually broken down.

The second influence has been the effect of the affidavit system on ties of kinship and patronage. Such personal sponsorship of one kind or another would have played an important part anyway in the Cypriot migration, but the 'affidavit system' made this a formal requirement. Indeed, it effectively limited the opportunity of migration to those who already had a close kinsman or co-villager in Britain, who was in a position to provide the necessary guarantees. This effect of the affidavit system in promoting ties of kinship and patronage among the migrants continued despite the administrative shortcomings of its later years until 1959 when the system was discontinued. Only in the peak period of migration that followed does it seem that unsponsored migration was widespread. This change was short-lived, however, because in 1962 a new set of controls impinged upon Cypriot migrants, this time imposed at the British end, but with a similar effect to that of the affidavit system. British Government control therefore pertains only to the tail-end of the migration, the period following the implementation of the Commonwealth Immigrants Act in mid-1962. Prior to that date, Cypriots, like all other Commonwealth citizens, had been free to enter Britain at will. The Act introduced a requirement that anyone wishing to enter Britain for the purpose of employment must be a holder of an employment voucher issued by the British Ministry of Labour. There were three categories of vouchers, A, B and C.[19] The figures for Cypriot applications for the respective vouchers, and also for the number issued, are of particular interest as they indicate the effect of this legislation on the sponsorship element in Cypriot migration. Between 1962 and 1966, some 90 per cent of Cypriot applicants were for Category A vouchers (coming to a specific job) as were 90 per cent of the vouchers actually issued to Cypriots. Given that only 13 per cent of all applicants for Commonwealth citizens fell into this category (and 30 per cent of the issues) this indicates a remarkable preponderance of sponsorship in Cypriot migrants. This figure could be misleading, however, for the issue of Category C vouchers was discontinued early on, leaving Category A (disregarding Category B for which less than 1 per cent of Cypriot applicants were qualified) as the sole category for which the mass of prospective Cypriot migrants were eligible. Even for the first six months of the Act's operation, however, 69 per cent of applications were for vouchers in Category A. This suggests that a good two-thirds of Cypriot migrants made use of informal sponsorship ties, even when there were no particular official pressures in this direction. However, the discontinuation of Category C vouchers, for which some 30 per cent of Cypriot applicants were hoping in the first half-year of the Act's operation, clearly excluded a substantial minority of potential Cypriot migrants who proposed to travel apparently independently of sponsorship at the British end. To this extent therefore it seems that the British immigration controls, like those of the Cyprus Government, operated so as to reinforce the advantage of potential migrants who already possessed relatives or friends in Britain who could meet the necessary requirements on their behalf. Conversely, after the Category C issue was discontinued, it became well-nigh impossible for Cypriots without such contacts to gain entry to Britain for settlement in accordance with the Act.

Government regulations are, therefore, an organisational framework of a migration providing for it a bureaucratic structure at a secondary level, but in such a way as to have an important influence on its primary level structure, that of family, kinship and patronage. Although the latter are traditional features of Cypriot society, here applied to the novel exigencies of migration overseas, the effect of the official system for migration control has been to promote on the one hand support for the family basis of the migration and on the other emphasis on the sponsorship element in the migration process.

Conclusion

The migration of Cypriots to Britain during the post-war period needs to be understood not as an aggregate movement of individuals, as is represented in the migration statistics, but as a socially organised process whereby individuals move both in relation to membership of family and kinship units as well as to ties of patronage. The traditional Cypriot patterns of family, kinship and patronage have been spontaneously deployed but also prompted through government regulation. These processes have combined to ensure a relatively cohesive primary structure of supportive relationships in Cypriot migration to Britain. They have helped to maintain the continuity of relationships between Cypriot emigrants and those who have remained behind, and also to the development of a cohesive and well-organised Cypriot community in Britain.

2

The Mirpuri migration from the north of Pakistan, discussed in this paper, is another case of first generation migrants from rural backgrounds who have followed a process of chain migration. Mirpuris, however, come from a non-European and Muslim culture, and they are perceived by the British as members of a 'black' minority.

This paper deals with the stresses of the migration process. It looks at the traditional setting in the homeland and at elements of support and stress in relationships in the village. These provide the starting point for the subsequent experiences of migration to, and settlement in, Britain. The processes of migration and settlement cause particular forms of stress in the mind of the migrant and in the forms of social interaction and style of life demanded by the new setting.

The paper illustrates that support and stress may mean different things in different cultures; that they are situation specific and that they change over time. Traditional systems of support may be strengthened to facilitate adjustment to life in Britain. But if in the short term they are supportive, these same mechanisms over time may prove major causes of stress.

Migration and Social Stress

Mirpuris in Bradford

Verity Saifullah Khan

The social stresses experienced by Pakistani migrants in Britain derive from three main 'arenas'; the traditional culture and emigration area; the migration process; and settlement in the new environment and society. The stresses experienced by ethnic minorities are not due to migration alone. The migration process itself is determined by features in the emigration area, the structure of the host society and the connections between the two. After a general introduction into the Pakistani population in Bradford this paper[1] outlines areas of stress in the emigration area and the traditional culture. It then considers the types of stress which are produced by the migration process and the process of settling into a new environment.

The paper illustrates that stress of differing types and intensity exists prior to migration. Certain traditional sources of stress emanate from the nature of village life, inter-personal relations, family structure and/or the socio-economic situation in the country. These may not be capable of resolution but only modification within the usual scheme of things. They may be carried with the migrant, or re-emerge in the migrant settlement and there become exacerbated, but alternatively the migration may solve the stress more effectively than otherwise possible. There are also the very immediate and personal experiences of stress which are related to the movement of the migrant from one social world to another. The support of traditional institutions of village life which re-emerge in modified form in Britain, help fellow migrants to cope with these experiences and those of the settlement process. But the two-sided nature of stress is evident in many examples quoted in the paper. The migration process itself is symbolic of this repeated dilemma; in an attempt to resolve certain hardships or provide a better future for his children the migrant produces new and often as stressful experiences.

Pakistanis in Bradford

There are approximately 30,000 Pakistanis in Bradford out of a total population of 300,000. Compared with other industrial cities in Britain Bradford has the highest percentage of Pakistanis among its Asian population. As in other northern cities, the majority of Pakistanis come from rural areas in the north of Pakistan. The majority of these in Bradford, and in the country at large, come from the following areas: Mirpur, a District of Azad Kashmir; Campbellpur, a District of Punjab Province; other Districts of Punjab Province (for example, Lyallpur, Sargodha, Jhelum and Rawalpindi Districts); and the North-west Frontier Province. All but the last category are Punjabi in culture, and speak some form of Punjabi. Villagers from the North-west Frontier Province, of whom there are relatively few in Britain, are Pathans and speak Pushto. Pakistanis from the cities and some educated villagers speak Urdu, the national language (Saifullah Khan, 1976c).

This paper restricts itself to the Mirpuri section of the Pakistani population in Bradford, which is possibly 60–70 per cent of the total. Mirpuris, like Campbellpuris and Sylhetis from Bangla Desh, are probably among the most encapsulated and home-orientated of Asian migrants in Britain. Contrary to the popular view these (and most) migrants are not the poorest of villagers, nor are they from the least fertile of areas. But compared to many Sikhs, Gujeratis and other Indians and Pakistanis in Britain, Mirpuris, Campbellpuris and Sylhetis come from relatively poor agricultural areas; they also tend to be more traditional and less educated than other Asian migrants.

The village-kin network is strong among Mirpuris and must be conceptualised as an extension of that in the homeland, but it is subject to new and considerable changes in the British context. Many Mirpuris in Bradford have minimal contact with the indigenous population. Men working in the textile industry, for example, work long hours on all-Pakistani night shifts. The little time available for relaxation is invariably spent with friends and kin in Bradford or other towns. Most Mirpuri women do not go out to work, because it is unacceptable in Islam and against the cultural tradition, and thus subject to severe criticism, and because many families still have young children and there are no close family members with whom children could be left. Women living in a neighbourhood with a high percentage of Pakistanis visit nearby friends or relatives and shop in Pakistani shops. Contact with the local population is limited to visits to the supermarket, post office, clinics and other relatively impersonal and official settings. Most children do not attend any play-group or nursery (due to lack of provision) and go straight to a special language centre for half a year to one-and-a-half years for their first experience of schooling. From here they move into mainstream schools of a totally English environment and often they are bussed some distance from their home locality.

Although many Mirpuris have stayed in Britain more years than they initially intended and have brought their families to join them, they have maintained contact and allegiance to the rest of the family and kin group (*biradari*) in the homeland and have not altered their plan to return home to Pakistan. Over time there has been an increasing appreciation of certain facilities and aspects of British life which are lacking in Pakistan. There is also an increased awareness of prejudice and discrimination by the majority British society and its 'corrupting' influence on children growing up in Britain.

Mirpur and the Village

The first arena that determines stresses experienced by Mirpuri migrants in their move to Britain, is the arena of the emigration area and traditional culture. This section outlines some of the main features of the homeland and local culture and thus points to the likely changes to be experienced by the migrant arriving and settling in urban Britain.

The homeland

The Mirpuris in Bradford come from Mirpur District of the part of Kashmir held by Pakistan, known as Azad (free) Kashmir. Although subjects of the Old State of Jammu and Kashmir, Mirpuris are citizens of Pakistan and are essentially Punjabi in culture, speaking a dialect of the Punjabi tongue. Mirpur District of Azad Kashmir lies to the north of the Punjab and, as in Campbellpur and the other bordering districts of the Punjab, the land is rain-fed, less fertile, and divided into smaller holdings than the more fertile, irrigated lands of Southern Punjab. Mirpur is, however, peculiar in certain significant ways. The land is hillier than the Punjab to the south; it does not have any important through communication route and it has been subject to particularly harsh regimes in past centuries which have delayed the educational, social and agricultural development evident in other areas of the sub-continent. Like other border areas Mirpur experienced the upheavals of Partition and many people moved to Mirpur from Indian-occupied Kashmir.

There has always been a tradition of migration from Mirpur. It is part of the general movement of population from northern mountain areas to the more fertile plains of the sub-continent, but migration has, no doubt, been increased by the harsh history and the subsequent backwardness of the country. Mirpuris were also subject to the general rural–urban migration in Pakistan which increased in this century with improved transportation and urbanisation. Some Mirpuris settled in southern cities may have joined the plantation labour migrations at the end of the nineteenth century and joined the Merchant Navy during the First World War. During the Second World War many men joined the British Army and Navy (Tinker, 1974, 1977) and since then Mirpur, with certain districts of the Punjab, has remained the major recruiting area for the Pakistan Army. Therefore, although the emigration of large numbers to Britain in the 1950s and 1960s had a particularly dramatic effect, Mirpur prior to this time had not been isolated from the outside world.

The building of Mangla Dam, a unique phenomenon of the 1960s, was a further cause of movement of population within Mirpur (approximately 100,000 people were displaced), and an impetus for some to try their luck in Britain. The building of a new city at the side of the lake, to replace old Mirpur city, attracted labour first for construction work and then for the construction of town houses on the surrounding expanse of underdeveloped land. The migration to Britain was well under way prior to the building of Mangla Dam. Many of the displaced persons were disrupted or in possession of a lump cash sum (of compensation money) and could take advantage of such an option.

Village life in the Indian sub-continent is neither isolated nor static. The gradual adaptation in past decades indicates the strength of traditional institutions rather than the absence of outside influence. The extension of communications, transportation, electricity, consumer items and a cash economy has affected all but the remotest areas. Large new houses have been built on the edge of villages with money from remittances and land has changed hands for new constructions and farming. This influx of capital and investment in the villages is undermining the traditional power structure. Dependent tenant farmers have become independent landowners with access to a continuous supply of capital. Some traditional landowners have sold land to these newly rich villagers and some have sent sons abroad to ensure access to the new sources of wealth and prestige. The flow of money, the sale of land and the contact with urban life both in Pakistan and the West has increased. Many migrants to Britain were small landowners and they invariably joined a relative or close friend in Britain with whom they were already in contact. The absence of many menfolk inevitably altered the village scene, but the joint family system and community life ensured support and minimal disruption.

The maintenance and even strengthening of certain features of Mirpur village life in the British setting indicate that the emigration to Britain is a new stage in the gradual adaptation to external influences and new options. The earliest pioneer migrants may have been exceptional in character, entrepreneurial and adventurous in spirit, but as the chain migration developed, ordinary villagers contemplated emigration. A journey to Britain was but one of several options open to villagers with contacts abroad and limited opportunities at home.

Many of these social and economic changes in the emigration area were not as disruptive as might be expected because they formed part of a wider series of changes that had been going on for many decades. The strength of the traditional institutions of family and kin (see below, pp. 44–5) lie in their flexibility and adaptability in times of separation and difficulty. But over time some of the changes have been a source of stress and uncertainty for certain individuals or sections of the village population. For example, investment in land and houses, remittances to family members and return visits of migrants are sources of wealth for the area and some of the inhabitants. Its uneven distribution, however, disrupts the status quo and causes tensions and jealousies between individuals, families and villagers. Some migrants do not meet the expectations of their families or kin group (*biradari*) and some are more successful than others. Awareness of alternative life-styles and resources may deepen the villagers feelings of deprivation and initially the information received from abroad produces a distorted, invariably idealised picture of life in Britain. Hopes and expectations are raised and the allegiance and expected return of migrants from Britain remain unquestioned. Some relatives hope to benefit from the success of *biradari* members, and others compete to marry offspring into families with migrant members. A family's claim to benefit, in financial and prestige terms, from the success of their migrant son does not necessarily decrease as time passes. As the migration developed, the establishment of travel agents, banks, concessionary rates and a direct air route facilitated return visits and a continued communication network through which straying migrants could be reminded of their loyalties and news of unacceptable behaviour could reach home.

The political instability of Azad Kashmir has also affected its economic development and future prospects. The general unemployment and the economic and political situation in the country are not encouraging for the potential businessman or for the family planning to return from life in the West. The rigid class structure of Pakistani society and the animosity felt for those from poorer, marginal areas, restricts the self-made Mirpuri's access to the urban Punjabi middle class. Life in rural areas is one of insecurity, hard toil and lack of good medical and educational facilities for all but the rich landowners who have access and transport to urban areas. Migrants planning to return to settle have to consider the relative advantages and disadvantages of life in Mirpur or elsewhere in Pakistan, as well as those of life in Britain.

Stress and support in the village[2]

The conditions and opportunities in the emigration area of the homeland determine, in part, the reaction of the migrant on his arrival in Britain. The migrant's subsequent reassessment of the opportunities and constraints in both England and Pakistan influences his degree of identification and involvement (both emotional and financial) with each country. The nature of traditional relationships in the villages of Mirpur is another crucial factor in our understanding of the migrant's perception of, and reaction to, the new land. It determines the skills and handicaps the migrant brings to his new situation in Britain. But an understanding of the traditional relationships and institutions of village life also helps us to evaluate the positive and negative effects of migration as perceived by the migrants. It is important to know the traditional areas of stress and their usual means of modification or resolution in the village setting, before one can assess the significance of the move to Britain. This move may involve physical separation from a typically stressful relationship (such as daughter-in-law and mother-in-law). Or the loss of typically supportive members of one's family or kin in the process of migration may mean that the new stresses experienced in settlement are increased. Alternatively traditional supportive systems or relationships that remain intact on migration may take up new functions, buffering stresses caused by the new situation in Britain.

In village society the individual is the centre of a complex network of rights and duties, which extend outwards from his/her immediate family to that of kin and fellow villagers. He or she is not an individual agent acting on his/her own behalf; his/her reputation depends on theirs and on the fulfilment of the obligations ascribed to his/her position at any particular time. The individualism and independence so valued in the West appears selfish and irresponsible to a Pakistani who expects and values the elements of dependency and loyalty in a relationship. An individual's rights and duties, specific to every relationship, are dictated by his/her age, sex, order of birth and others living or present. The main features of such inter-personal relationships are the hierarchy or 'pecking-order', the authority of elders and the public authority of men and deference of women. Family and kin take priority over individual preference, and trust and loyalty decreases with the distance from the family core.

Relationships within the family are close, emotional, dependent; they are relationships of loyalty and obligation. Subject to restricted interaction between the sexes and deference shown to elders, relationships in the village are personal, face-to-face interactions. Village life is outdoor and gregarious, everyone knowing everyone else. The village is a moral arena in which reputations are assessed and re-assessed, and potential deviants pulled back into line. All interactions are based on the model of family relationships. Close friends are classified as 'sister' or 'brother' and the relationship gradually acquires the interdependency and loyalty typical of siblings.

The advantages of the sociability and collectivity of village life are balanced by the intensity of disputes when they arise, the pressure to conform, the harsh treatment of deviants and the potentially malicious role of gossip. In impersonal, bureaucratic and formal interactions, a villager, while utilising terms and actions of deference, may employ praise (to his 'elder' or 'wiser') or suggest a distant blood or friendship tie to sway the decision in his favour. He is unused to highly bureaucratised and formal settings. The mechanics of the situation are alien to him and he is unskilled in informal, matter-of-fact, distance-maintaining interaction typical of urban and Western lifestyles. The importance attributed to privacy, emotional restraint and self-containment in English society is also alien to the Mirpuri. It is the known and the related who are trusted. However, in new settings away from 'home', the boundary of this in-group extends to fellow countrymen or men from the home district. Therefore, when the first pioneer migrants settled in Britain, they often shared households and established close supportive relationships with non-Mirpuris, but fellow Pakistanis or other South Asians (Dahya, 1973, 1974).

The village household is frequently a three-generational unit comprising grandparent(s), married son(s) and their wives and children, unmarried sons and daughters and sometimes an unmarried, divorced or widowed uncle or aunt. Daughters move to their husband's family on marriage. Property is held in common and resources pooled whether derived from work on the land or wage-labour. Decisions are made communally but final authority rests with the head of the household, the eldest male. Authority is allocated according to gender (men have more authority than women), and age (elders have more authority than their juniors). The closest bonds of friendship and emotional attachment are within the family and close kin, and are frequently stronger between those who are clearly differentiated by age, generation or gender. Relationships of stress are more likely between those who occupy similar and thus competitive positions. Within the family and kin there is potential conflict over authority, respect and the affection of significant others. For example, the wives of two brothers, and the unmarried sister and new wife of her brother often have stress-ridden relationships. The mother-in-law/daughter-in-law relationship is fraught with problems as the new bride adapts to a husband and a new family, and the mother-in-law concedes to share the affections of her son. On the death of the male head of the family the new fraternal joint family is structurally weak, the two sons and their two wives being in potentially equal positions.

The pre-ordained clear-cut rules and roles of the family unit contribute to a certain stability and psychological health, but do not prepare the members for change beyond that of the natural development cycle of the family. The interdependence and warmth of relationships buffers hardships and external threat but the stability and control exercised by the unit demands a restraint on individual initiative and independence which the more independent of mind are likely to resist. Those who voluntarily or involuntarily deviate from the norm (for example, widows, the physically deformed) are subject to particularly severe reprimand or control. Those believed vulnerable (for example, young unmarried girls) are controlled and those who, by force or choice, do not fulfil the expected life-cycle course (of marriage, bearing children, for example) lose esteem and influence. In both these cases it is not only the individual whose reputation is blemished, but he or she jeopardises the reputation of the whole family or kin group. Those who deviate from the norm thus place themselves in potentially stressful situations. For example those of independent mind will be pressurised into conforming and thus be subject to considerable tension. When people who prefer celibacy are forced to marry, their marriages are likely to be unhappy, at least initially. This may also result when political and/or financial considerations take precedence over likely personal compatibilities or when parents have little bargaining power or choice over their offspring's spouse (for example, due to poverty or the physical unattractiveness or deformity of their child).

Beyond the household it is the kin group (*biradari*) that regulates and structures relationships. The *biradari* ('brotherhood') is an endogamous group whose members claim descent in the paternal line from a common male ancestor. *Biradari* elders are respected and have power to ensure the cohesion of the group by reprimanding deviants and so maintaining the *izzat* (prestige) of the group. Membership of a *biradari* defines an individual's rights and duties, sentiments and general conduct. There is a strong sense of belonging and psychological security which relates to the warmth of relationships and the way the *biradari* functions as a welfare, banking and advice service. The system of gift exchange gives financial support to *biradari* families in times of considerable expenditure (for example when a child is born or a son/daughter is married) and expresses official alignment and solidarity with other households. It forms a crucial supportive system for relatively poor villagers under economic stress, living in a country with no welfare system and with limited medical facilities.

However, interaction between *biradari* members is not always harmonious. They sometimes bicker or fight, and at times a serious prolonged rift may develop between two families or factions. People also strike up particular friendships within the group and care has to be taken not to demonstrate indifference to the less friendly of members, and to avoid shaming poorer members by giving presents too large for them to reciprocate.

The migration process

The migration process is a major cause of stress in itself. Two related reasons are outlined in this section. The first is determined by the migrant's ideology. The changing expectations and re-assessment of self produced by the migration process is further confused by the varying degrees of social change in the two countries in which the migrant belongs and feels he belongs to differing degrees. The second cause of stress is that of separation and divided families which means that different members of a family have different experiences, orientation and participation in the two worlds of the migrant.

The migrant ideology and social change

Until recent years the intending migrant had an idealised picture of a land of wealth and security where a fortune could be amassed, with minimum effort. *Vilayat* (Britain) was pictured as a great and rich land, a land of promise and a way to solve all one's problems. Those who came back from *vilayat* returned, in the villagers' terms, with money, knowledge and stories of their experience and acquisitions. They brought prestige to their families and a greater security in the form of new land or a house. Their decision to leave for *vilayat* was not an individual decision, but one made by the family and perceived as an investment for them all. The migrant left home therefore highly motivated with many expectations, but also many obligations. He planned to earn as much money as possible as soon as possible and then to return home with the means to improve his family's socioeconomic position and hopes for the future. These expectations and incumbent obligations explain the one-sided feed-back which maintained a positive and desired view of *vilayat* among the villagers, and their corresponding lack of understanding of daily life in Britain; the hard work and inevitable problems that were involved. As a matter of pride the migrant does not wish to admit to his kin at home the initial difficulties he faced, nor that his progress is slow. He is unable to save as fast as he expected, and over time – and with a gradual change in his assessment of the amount of money needed to return – he prolongs the date of his departure from England. Even when he calls his family to Britain he maintains the plan to return one day. The strength of this 'myth of return' (as it is called because it is so rarely realised) reflects the strength of emotional ties with distant family and kin, but also the need for firm roots and the justification for past hardships. The initial aim of migration was to return to settle in prosperous style. To abandon it after many hardships and sacrifices renders the initial move meaningless and publicises a curtailment of traditional loyalties and allegiances. As time passes the migrant becomes used to certain aspects of life in Britain and although he is frequently unaware of it, his aspirations and expectations (of, for example, an adequate standard of living or a satisfactory education for his children) are gradually changing. In the first few years in Britain he has often felt considerable stress due to the separation from his family, the new climate, a monotonous job and many other difficulties. Over time he becomes increasingly aware of his inferior social position in relation to British society and amongst other Pakistanis. He is likely to feel that the only acknowledgement of the hardships he has faced, and the only place he will feel an improved social standard, is back home in Mirpur.

Facing these various stresses the migrant in Britain idealises the village world. This means that when he does return to Pakistan to visit his family, or look into the possibility of setting up a business to return to, he faces a new set of disillusionments. It is only when the migrant returns home to Mirpur that he realises his changed aspirations and attitudes. Although delighted by the reception from family and kin and the newly acquired status, many migrants are soon depressed by the conditions of life and financial and family pressures, and begin to question their plan to return to settle with their family. While re-establishing contact with his family and kin, he begins to realise the difficulties he and his family would experience if he did return to settle. Therefore, on returning to Britain the migrant is likely to become more involved and orientated to his future life in Bradford and, although never renouncing his ties with the homeland, such visits help in a more realistic assessment of the alternatives available to him. The migrant remains dependent on both worlds; in one he has achieved economic advancement and in the other he is accorded recognition of his success. Physically restricted to one world he lives totally in neither.

The physical movement between these two worlds and the ongoing emotional attachment to the homeland produces another form of stress, which relates essentially to the different rates of social change in both countries. Even rural migrants moving to cities in Pakistan are subject to stress, but it is inevitably more intense in a movement from rural Mirpur to a Western city. This involves telescoping two major movements into one: the movement from a rural to an urban area and that from east to west. Certain sections of the urban population in Pakistan are exposed to considerable westernisation and modernisation and thus migrants to Britain from this background are better prepared and face fewer stresses on arrival (Jeffrey, 1976). This faster rate of social change in Pakistan's urban areas has produced (relative to village life) a greater generation gap. Educational facilities and later marriage have extended (perhaps created) the period of 'adolescence'. The urban middle class in Pakistan are in fact facing many of the stresses experienced by Mirpuri villagers when they migrate abroad. But Mirpuri villagers are not aware of this. Many have arrived in Britain direct from village life and not until they visit urban Pakistan on a return trip do they realise this alternative perspective. In Britain they tend to interpret the problems and stresses experienced as a direct result of life in Britain, and not as an inevitable feature of an urban society under rapid social change.

It was shown in the section on the homeland that emigration areas in the sub-continent are often subject to more rapid social and economic change than many other rural areas. This is due to the movement of population and access to new resources, etc. Migrants resident abroad are often unaware of these changes in the homeland and, as has often been remarked, the settlement abroad may be more traditional than that of the emigration area. This is not due solely to lack of involvement in the home society, but also to the position of a minority that feels insecure and under threat from the majority (both politically and culturally). Thus migration may catalyse change in the emigration area, but slow down changes in the immigrant settlement abroad.

Separation and social skills

Migrants are frequently permanently or temporarily separated from their families and their members are therefore subject not only to different experiences, but to these different rates of social change. The number of divided Mirpuri families remains large and consists of those who intend to remain divided for a certain period of time and those who are planning or attempting to re-unite. For both categories, and sections of the family in both countries, there are many difficulties and ramifications. For example, we have already seen that the Mirpuri villager does not possess the social skills or the documentation demanded by a complex bureaucratic system. This has led to exploitation by intermediary agents and the creation of a black market in the required forms and certificates. As a result many migrants, exercising their legal right to settle in Britain, obtain false documentation and commit themselves to penalisation if their genuine case is questioned. The resultant anxiety, the months of waiting for appointments, the deferring of decisions, the travelling and expense involved and the overall uncertainty and inability to plan causes great stress to many divided families (Akram, 1974). Communication between spouses, and between parents and siblings, is frequently hindered by the inability of one party to write letters and the necessity for communication through a third party. The disappointments and dismay caused by refusals, the difficulties of organising an appeal, and the anxiety produced by the actual interviews and cross-checking are remembered and told to others. The humiliations, the long periods of uncertainties and the experience of increasingly restrictive immigration control has influenced many others to call dependants now in the hope of avoiding greater harassment and a permanently enforced division of their families in the future (Birmingham CDP, 1977).

One particular circumstance of stress for migrants is the family crisis which is exacerbated when family and kin are physically separated. Death in the family in Britain or Pakistan is particularly distressful because it is a time when family and kin unite and support the bereaved and because distant family members are sometimes unaware of a likely demise. Death or illness in the village family can cause an extended separation of household members in Britain. Fathers or mothers may need to return to Pakistan for months and occasionally years at a time and children left in Britain may find this particularly stressful.

Another area of stress arises from the husbands' and wives' different degree of access to, and understanding of, the wider society. In Bradford both husband and wife may have minimum contact with the indigenous population. The husband, following the traditional scheme of things, usually maintains responsibility for business affairs with the help of literate friends or Pakistani businessmen. The husband's greater knowledge and facility in dealing with the outside world is not necessarily a source of disruption, but it is likely to involve changing attitudes and aspirations which may introduce tensions and misunderstandings. This is particularly likely when a husband has lived for several or many years in Britain prior to calling his family to Britain. In extreme cases the husband's re-appraisal of values and preferences, or his inflated view of his achievements and status leads him to divorce or maintain his physical separation from his wife.

A more serious imbalance in the conjugal relationship will be evident in a greater number of cases, as newly married men come to join their wives or fiancées in Britain. Such an arrangement is prone to even greater stress than that of the new bride joining her husband. It conflicts with the established pattern of public male authority and knowledge of the outside world and the greater adaptation demanded of the bride. If the marriage is organised within the *biradari* it is likely that the husband will have a limited command of English, and very little confidence in or experience of an urban environment.

There are other examples of fundamental threat to the traditional hierarchy of authority and respect accorded to members of a family or household. These are not due to prolonged separation, or totally diverse pasts, but to the different lengths of time spent in Britain and related to this, the degree of access to the outside, wider society. Young adult men who arrived at the age of eighteen or nineteen, six or ten years ago, or as sons who have had the last four or five years of British schooling are likely to know more of the English language, local culture and national scene, relative to their fathers or uncles. Similarly children who were born in Britain or have undergone most of their schooling in this country have a greater facility in communication than their parents. Elders may feel threatened or insecure, and although many minors maintain the public authority and respect due to elders, occasions arise when minors publicly question or disobey their elders. It is on such occasions that parents glimpse the fundamental influence a British education may have on their children (see C. Ballard, this volume).

The divergent culture and orientation of British-born Mirpuris and their parents produces tensions that arise from a mutual inability to appreciate the priorities and preoccupations of the other. The generation gap is wide and is deepened because the two generations participate in differing degrees in the three social arenas; the homeland, the local Pakistani world in Bradford, and the majority society in Britain. Their differing social skills determine access to English society and this, in conjunction with their differing values and orientation, determines their degree of understanding of the local society in Bradford and in Mirpur.

The settlement process

Settling into a new environment and meeting people of a different culture, often for the first time, involves many forms of stress. The necessary linguistic and other social skills to enable communication with neighbours and workmates have to be acquired by the Mirpuri in Britain. The radical change in environment and the preoccupations and worries of the target migrant do not provide the confidence or the time to mix with and understand the local population and their culture. The migrant's disillusionments and difficulties and his experience of discrimination from the local population and fellow (non-Mirpuri) Pakistanis deter the take-up of certain opportunities when they do arise. This section illustrates the kinds of stress which emerge from conditions of the new environment and which combine with cultural preferences to bring new meaning to certain features of the tradtitional culture. It then argues that while many of the features of the traditional culture which facilitate settlement are supportive in the short term, they are major causes of stress in the long run.

Confronting the new environment

Significant environmental sources of stress are the new climate and living conditions in Britain. They have serious consequences for the emotional and physical health of Mirpuris. Most Mirpuris are pleased to avoid the hottest weather of the Pakistan summer, but find the winters in Britain bitterly cold and the climate generally dull and depressing. The climate and type of housing combine to impose an indoor life-style, restricted in space and frequency of social inter-action, which markedly contrasts with the outdoor sociability of the family, courtyard and village. The new climate demands thicker and more numerous layers of clothing and nappies for children. Besides the discomfort of wearing socks and closed shoes, the new clothing demands more washing and drying in a land with no physical help or companionship and little sunshine. Rain and cold weather force children to play in restricted space indoors without supervision from other family members. In Britain, therefore, the mother is in sole charge of her children during most of the day.

The new climate, the lack of sunshine and limited outdoor activity can be detrimental to health, particularly for women restricted by custom and necessity to the house. The higher incidence of osteomalacia, rickets and anaemia found among some Asian popu-lations in Britain is partly due to the unsuitability of a diet well suited to a different life-style and climate (Hunt, 1976, 1977).

The impersonality and large scale of city life is striking to those who have come direct from rural Mirpur. Lack of facility in English and English mannerisms hinder communication and increase the likeli-hood of misunderstanding. Formal interactions, complex bureau-cracy, the demand for punctuality and the faster pace of industrial urban life can cause underlying pressure and anxiety. Men in the village in Mirpur worked in the fields or at their traditional occu-pation, but they returned at certain times during the day and were at hand in times of crisis. In Britain work is separated from the family, often far from the home and for long night-shifts. Many women do not know where their husbands' factories or mills are situated, and are unable to get in touch with them at work. Many have to adjust to being on their own for long hours for the first time in their lives. In such circumstances it is easier for the women if several Pakistani families or couples share one house, and if there are other Pakistani families resident in the same neighbourhood.

The urban industrial environment means that many men have to adjust to the new demands of industrial wage-labour. Unlike many other institutions of village life which are evident in the Mirpuri's daily life in Bradford, the new economic activity bears, for most Mir-puris, no relation to their past work experience. In the mills and factories of Bradford work is not defined and regulated by the worker. There is a strict routine, regularity, uniformity and repetitiveness in the work. Initially the villager, thinking in terms of the home society, is appreciative of a large pay packet, but over time he realises the higher cost of living, and comes to hear about higher wages paid for equivalent kinds of work. Some men, depending on their age and health, become physically exhausted and depressed by the long hours worked, and the monotony and physical conditions of the workplace. Shift work ignores bodily rhythms, affects sleep patterns and alters the usual pattern of family life, and may cause serious areas of tension within the family unit. Fathers may, however, see just as much (or as little) of their children when they work on night-shifts. And for those men who can manage with less sleep, working 'nights' enables them to cope with bank and office business, etc. during the day. For all the long-term disadvantages of ethnic work groups, they do allow company and support at work, avoidance of tension with white or West Indian workers, less surveillance and more economic travel arrangements.

This new type of economic activity is separated from the household unit, and in addition to the large scale and diversity of an urban population, it causes Mirpuri women to be subject to a stricter form of *purdah* than they experienced in the home village (Saifullah Khan, 1975, 1976a, 1976b). Mirpuri women contribute less to, and have less control over, the household income in Britain. In the village they collected water from the village well, looked after domestic animals, and participated in certain agricultural and farming activities. In this essentially subsistence economy they contributed directly to the household income, but also controlled the distribution and use of incoming produce. In Bradford they are more dependent on their husbands, not only for household and personal finances, but also emotionally. Women spend a lot of time on their own and do not have access to, or the support of, their natal family and close friends when stress emerges in the marital relationship. Besides shopping in local Pakistani shops there are fewer reasons to go outside and greater chance of interacting with unknown men. Observance of the principle that women should not go out to work is ensured by the size of the Mirpuri population: its close-knit networks and fast internal communication causes pressure to conform. Many Mirpuri women argue that they should not work, at least while they are bringing up their family. But an increasing number express the wish to go to work for financial and/or companionship reasons (Saifullah Khan, 1979). There are no ethnic or religious organisations which encourage the participation of women or provide a meeting place – like, for example, the Gurdwara for Sikh women.[3] So Mirpuri women are dependent on their own information and resource network which is more likely to be utilised than official agencies of the host society (partly because of trust accorded to the known and personal contact and partly because of inability and a perceived hostility or indifference on the part of the majority society).

The nature of the migration process and features of the new environment also bring new meaning to the traditional family system in Britain. Both men and women speak of the advantages and disadvantages of the new situation and even though some of the adaptations initially cause considerable stress many admit that the new and positive aspects will make it difficult for them to return to live in the old style in the homeland. For example some men and women who have previously lived in a joint household find the sudden independence and responsibilities of life in Britain a great anxiety. For others, or at a later period, the compensations of a new-found freedom are realised; greater privacy and time together, and full control over the running of the household and socialisation of the children. Many women are pleased to get away from their mothers-in-law or other interfering relatives despite the added work load and many suggest that they could never return to Pakistan and live jointly. The greater time and privacy available to a young married couple hastens a companionship typical only of elderly couples in the village. But this change indicates a future tension; that of elderly retired parents living with sons in Britain. Children educated in Britain are likely to retain the respect and loyalty due to elderly parents, but many young couples are used to, or value, a greater independence than that enjoyed in joint family living. However, the prevailing economic and housing situations are likely to be factors working towards the maintenance of this highly economic unit as more first-generation migrants reach retiring age and their children marry.

Change over time

Although there were small settlements of Pakistanis in Bradford from the 1940s onwards, the majority of Pakistani men arrived in the 1960s and have lived in Britain for eight to twenty years. Many Mirpuri men found work in Bradford in the declining industries which are characterised by low wages and a high percentage of night work.

Many men work on all-Pakistani night-shifts and work maximum overtime. These characteristics are in part due to the structure and inequalities of the industrial system and in part the actual or subsequent preference of workers to stick with their own kind (to avoid harassment and maximise the psychological and economic benefits of co-operation). But the nature of the migration process itself tended to support such encapsulation. Migrants came to join friends or relatives, they depended on their support and this directed them into certain occupations and life-styles. The natural tendency to trust and interact only with people of one's own village-kin network or home locality has increased in Britain as numbers have increased. Larger populations have in turn strengthened the pressure to conform and decreased access to alternative types of work and interaction with the indigenous population. Increasingly encapsulated in their own world, the skills required for communication and participation could not be acquired so easily and mutually rigid views and stereotypes developed to hinder (or justify) the segregation between the migrants and the majority society.

Although strengthened, modified and altered in significant ways, the main institutions of village life remain fundamental principles regulating daily life in Bradford. But over time the structure and reception of British society determined their development. Although encapsulated and thus protected for longer than some minorities, Mirpuris have gradually come into contact with and heard about many cases of prejudice and discrimination. The increase in unpleasant incidents and news of unfair treatment have coincided with an increased understanding of national affairs and the significance of certain incidents, such as National Front marches and Enoch Powell's speeches. The stress of these personal experiences and an actual or perceived insecurity due to uncertain legal status and an inferior social status tend to enhance the migrant's encapsulation and desire to return home. This trend co-exists with the greater appreciation and participation in certain aspects of the wider society as more families reunite and children grow up in this society.

These opposing forces and the changing impact of determinants both external and internal to the minority illustrate that there are many complex factors influencing the course of ethnic relations in Britain and the lives of Mirpuri parents and their children. The passage of time does not inevitably mean change towards the minorities' acceptance of indigenous culture and access to equal opportunities, and will certainly not be as rapid (in one or two generations) as is often assumed. While the initial settlement in Bradford by Mirpuri villagers was not a deliberate statement of resistance to adaptation (Saifullah Khan, 1976c) it is likely, especially in the present unemployment situation and political climate, that second-generation British-born Mirpuris will consciously demonstrate their allegiance to their community (or a wider Asian community), and links will be maintained with the homeland through marriage, visiting and the exchange of information and gifts.[4]

Summary

The stresses outlined in this paper are stresses experienced, at times articulated, and often manifest in the daily lives of Mirpuri families in Bradford. Focusing on both ends and the mechanics of the migration process counteracts the frequently held notion that stresses experienced by ethnic minorities are due to migration alone. Knowledge of the traditional culture and conditions in the homeland is necessary for a balanced evaluation of the effects of migration on the migrant's life-style and values. The stressful experience of migration is also frequently omitted from studies of ethnic minorities in Britain, but it is a crucial determinant of a migrant's perception of his situation, and the actual options open to him. While many of the supportive institutions of village life in the short term buffer confrontation with the new and alien world in Britain, in the long term they not only restrict access to it, but also hinder the attainment of things valued by the migrant.

This paper has illustrated that stress can have many sources and may be experienced and manifest in very different ways. Stress may be produced wholly by external factors beyond the individual's control and such factors may relate to physical and environmental conditions, the prevailing socio-economic situation and political and social factors. Any situation at a particular point in time involves a compound of such factors which are difficult to disentangle. Different individuals and different families react to the same external constraints in a variety of ways. This differential response to similar situations of stress is due in part to the different resources (economic, social, emotional, ideological, etc.) available to the family or individual, their ability to utilise them and the particular psychological make-up of the individual(s) involved. Both the migrant's resources and his liabilities can only be assessed if they are placed within a wide geographical framework (encompassing the homeland and Britain) and within the context of historical and social change.

3

This paper focuses on people who were not part of a mass chain migration. Although many West African couples in London come from relatively privileged backgrounds, the move to London is one which involves a loss of the traditionally supportive systems of the home society. How do these couples, in a radically different setting and with clear short-term objectives, divide their time and labour, care for their children and cope with the changed expectations of their relationship?

The paper concentrates on the stress experienced by husband and wife in their adjustment to new demands on their relationship brought by changes in the division of labour, the decision-making process and leisure patterns which are features of life in Britain. It points to an association between 'joint marital roles' and a relatively low degree of stress. If on the other hand a couple retains its traditional 'segregated' activity patterns on arrival in this country, and both have jobs or studies, then it is the wife who suffers from the loss of traditional forms of support. Because, for example, a high degree of co-operation is necessary many couples seek out-of-home forms of child care such as fostering.

In the eyes of the British these West African couples form a single category but the author illustrates crucial differences between Ashanti and Ibo culture which make the latter relatively more adaptable to the type of marital relationship demanded by their situation in London.

Stress in Marriage

West African couples in London

Esther Goody and Christine Muir Groothues

This paper focuses on the marital relationships of West African couples in London. Whereas traditional West African marital roles are sharply segregated, with each spouse responsible for separate spheres, and clearly defined areas of 'men's work' and 'women's work' – 'men's affairs' and 'women's affairs' – the model of the Western middle-class family, to which professional West Africans increasingly aspire, prescribes companionate marriage with sharing of both rights and responsibilities (see Oppong, 1974). This study was planned to allow the rating of each couple on the extent to which they defined their roles in various spheres as 'joint' or 'segregated'.[1] We were concerned to discover to what extent traditional role definitions had persisted in London, where both constraints of daily life and the 'Western' family model would tend to favour joint role structure. In selecting the couples for intensive study we chose half from a group with strong patrilineal descent institutions (the Ibo) and half from among a group whose traditional structure was matrilineal (the Ashanti) – both from West Africa. Such a contrast makes it possible to isolate which aspects of traditional social organisation are most closely related to the adaptation of conjugal roles in life in London.

The work on marital roles is part of a wider study of West African families in London which is concerned with the practice of sending young children to live with English foster parents. The fostering of older children with relatives is a recognised practice in West Africa. But in adapting this tradition to life in England, children are being fostered at a much younger age, and with strangers of a different linguistic and cultural group from their parents. The wider study tries to examine a number of factors which might be related to the early fostering of West African children in England. However the present paper explores only one dimension, that of marital roles, both in relation to traditional marital roles and in relation to fostering.[2]

In addition to looking at traditional marital roles and at current role structure, the third factor which we examine is stress in the performance of different aspects of marital roles. Role stress holds an ambiguous status. High stress scores appear in some cases to be related to the fact that a particular type of role definition does not 'work' in the conditions of life in London. In other cases high role stress appears to be related to the dissonance experienced between what spouses think should be happening and what is actually happening. And in some cases stress undoubtedly feeds back into the definition of marital roles themselves.

In looking at the associations between the various indices which follow, these should be seen as mainly descriptive and sometimes suggestive of more systematic relationships which might hold for other couples under similar circumstances.

Indices of marital relations

Ever since Bott (1957) suggested that there might be a significant difference in the pattern of marital relations with different styles of extra-familial networks, students of marital relations have looked for patterns of this kind.[3] Her categories were based on the extent to which a couple carried out the various activities of marriage and family life jointly, either taking turns or co-operating in the performance of some task, or whether their roles were segregated, each having a separate sphere of competence and responsibility. In her study of London families, Bott found that those couples whose pattern of task performance was segregated tended to spend their leisure time with kin or with friends of the same sex who knew one another. That is to say, their network was 'connected'; each spouse would depend on his or her own friends for assistance and support in the activities for which they were responsible, rather than turning to the other partner. Those couples whose activity pattern was primarily a joint one had mutual friends who were unknown to one another; their network was 'unconnected'. Further, they both tended to have the same people as friends. Thus friendship activities – dinners, outings – involved husband and wife together and jointness was carried over into the sphere of friendship. Husband and wife in couples of this type turned to one another for assistance in domestic activities rather than to kin or friends of the same sex outside the marital family.

When West African couples who have spent some time in Europe return home, they often mention that abroad they did everything together and lived quite a different life from the one they now find possible. Partly in order to test the validity of this retrospective view, a rough classification of the twenty families was undertaken in terms of the jointness or segregation of their marital roles in various spheres of activity. It is also important for an understanding of the division of labour within the domestic unit to assess the demands made on each partner by the presence of children. But there is a more general reason for enquiry into the way in which marital roles are defined by West Africans in the United Kingdom. For in West African societies the division of all spheres of activity into male and female is very strong. Even in the homes of some civil servants and professional men, meals are taken separately by man and wife, and many leisure activities are independently followed. The husband has his career, and the wife either has a career or some sort of a job which occupies her during the day. Their home is a common ground on which they share interests, above all, in their children. Other professional families do not follow this segregated pattern (Oppong, 1974) but it is a common one, and follows directly from the traditional distribution of tasks and spheres of competence between men and women. Thus in 'traditional' West African society, and still today to a notable extent, marital roles are highly segregated, both in terms of interests and task performance. With this as the base line, what kind of picture do we find among West African families in London? If it does differ from the situation in Africa, how and why does it do so?

In addition to looking at the degree of jointness or segregation of marital roles in the twenty couples, other aspects of behaviour have been assessed. On the basis of the notes kept on each family throughout the study, a rating was made of the areas in which stress had been observed and, very crudely, of its severity. After looking at the pattern within each ethnic group, the Ibo and Ashanti families are compared on selected indices.[4] Marital relations are then considered in relation to network connectedness and the intensity of interaction with kin and friends outside the family. Finally it is important to consider whether any, some, or all of these factors appear to be related to the decision to foster children while in London.

Marital role jointness: activity spheres

In making ratings of the degree to which a couple followed a joint pattern of role behaviour, it was necessary to distinguish a number of different activity spheres: domestic chores, leisure activities, finance, major decisions, parental roles and communication. Each of these in turn is based on several specific activities thus giving precision to the index. For instance, the index of jointness in 'domestic chores' includes ratings of the degree to which both spouses participate in household chores, shopping and the feeding and bathing of children. The index of jointness of parental role also includes the feeding and bathing of children, but in addition includes baby-sitting, discipline of children and the making of decisions about the children's future and so on. As can be seen from these examples, the indices overlap at some points and cannot be treated as independent. However this overlapping reflects the complexity of family roles and cannot realistically be avoided. Whether or not the same item is included in two indices the areas of activity themselves still merge at the edges.

Before considering any overall ranking for degree of jointness of marital role, each of the activity spheres is discussed briefly, and the pattern of rating for each of the two sets of couples is analysed.

Domestic chores

Neither group shows a tendency to share domestic chores, though there is one Ashanti couple and one Ibo couple who are strongly joint in this activity area. In considering these results it should be remembered that all but two of the wives are working, and sixteen out of twenty work full time. Despite this, most husbands help little if at all with domestic chores.

Finances

Analysis of the sharing of financial responsibility is complicated for these West African families by the fact that both husband and wife are earning. Thus in one sense the responsibility for supporting the family is shared in all these couples. However in several cases each spouse takes responsibility for certain aspects of running the household, and manages these independently of the other. This is what Bott has referred to as independent rather than joint conjugal role structure.[5]

In rating the Ashanti and Ibo couples for financial jointness, it is important to distinguish those who share in managing their financial affairs from others who operate as it were in a parallel but autonomous way. We have used two criteria for this index: the holding of a joint bank account, and the making together of decisions involving major expenditure.

Although about half of each group scores as 'mildly joint', there is hardly any overlap at the extremes. Ibo are more often truly joint, and Ashanti are more often truly segregated. All the Ibo couples we studied made joint decisions about major purchases, and four also held joint bank accounts. For the Ashanti, on the other hand, only one couple held a joint bank account, and several did not make financial decisions jointly. This difference between the two groups is one which occurs in other indices. Its implications will be considered later, but here it should be noted that the difference is not a function of whether wives are working. The only woman not working at all during 1971 was Ibo, and the one who temporarily stopped work was also Ibo. If there were a bias from women not working (which could seriously affect so small a sample), it should have the opposite effect to that observed. That is, one would expect that women who are not themselves earning, would be less likely to participate in financial affairs. Yet Ibo women all make financial decisions together with their husbands.

Decision-making

The field notes were rated in terms of whether decisions about husband's and wife's work and study, the children's future and the couple's future together were made jointly, or individually by those most directly concerned, or by the husband as the 'head of the household'. Here again the tendency for Ibo couples to make decisions together is apparent. The high proportion who fall at the 'joint' end of the scale is particularly striking since so many different kinds of decisions were considered in compiling the score, and since among these was the question of the husband's future plans, which is probably among the most difficult areas for men to share with their wives. Only two of the Ashanti couples said that they discussed the husband's plans together. But then the Ashanti couples reported fewer instances of discussing every type of decision together than did the Ibo. While unwillingness to decide things together can be seen as an extreme form of role segregation, in the contrast between these Ashanti and the Ibo couples it represents also a difference in commitment to a joint future. This point will be discussed further later, but clearly where a union is seen as subject to disruption, there are additional factors which each spouse may wish to take into account in making long-term decisions. Where a marriage is seen as permanent, interests are identified and all decisions affect both partners.

Leisure

Here we are concerned with whether a couple share their leisure activities, and also with whether they share in the responsibility for staying with children so that leisure activity away from home is possible. The familiar pattern of the relatively highly segregated roles of the Ashanti couples is even more exaggerated in this index, with only two couples sharing in the arrangement or enjoyment of leisure activities. The Ibo, on the other hand, almost exactly reverse the picture, with only three couples who do not share their leisure pursuits to some extent. It is interesting that the two Ashanti couples who do share in leisure do so in both senses which we considered. If this pattern were to be repeated for a larger sample it would suggest a 'quantum jump', i.e. that where an Ashanti couple structures marital roles jointly, it does so across the board and not only in minor ways. In the present context this is no more than speculation, but the point must be considered in relation to other material.

Parental roles

The structuring of parental roles was considered in relation to daily care (feeding and bathing), to discipline, and to decisions about the children's future. Here again the Ibo couples are conspicuously more 'joint' in their roles, with none of them appearing in the 'segregated' half of the scale, where half of the Ashanti couples are located. The difference between Ibo and Ashanti scores on this index cannot, however, be attributed to a general Ibo tendency to share in decision-making. All but two of the Ashanti couples made at least some decisions about their children's future together – indeed joint decisions were far more common for Ashanti couples in this area than in any other. Yet fully half of the Ashanti parents acted overall individually, without consulting one another, or left the other parent to cope most of the time. It must be stressed that this is not a matter of abdicating parental responsibilities. Rather, these are parents who act individually, in accord with the dictates of their various other responsibilities, instead of treating these tasks and problems as areas for joint management. It is only fair to note that only one of the Ibo couples dealt with all these areas jointly.

Communication and commitment

The final index is a measure of the jointness of marital roles. Under this heading the extent to which the couple appears to be committed to a joint future is considered. That is, whether they talk in terms of returning together to West Africa and of what they plan to do together on their return. We also considered here the level of communication which seems to obtain between husband and wife, whether they talk freely together or speak only when there is something specific which must be discussed or arranged.

Differences here are less than clear than on some of the other indices, but there is again a tendency for the Ashanti couples to be more segregated in their role behaviour. In particular there are three Ashanti couples who have very poor communications and do not plan in terms of a joint future, while there are no Ibo couples with this extreme degree of marital segregation. And while there are two Ashanti couples with the extreme joint score of '4' there are three Ibo couples in this category. It seems probable that by introducing a rating for level of communication we have added a largely psychological dimension to this index which to some extent cuts across the socially determined playing of marital roles. But the measures of commitment to a joint future, it is argued, are more a function of social factors than of personality. The results suggest that the Ibo couples are nearly all committed to a future together. They differ primarily in the degrees of their commitment. The Ashanti couples on the other hand, show a bimodal distribution, being committed either highly or not at all to plans which involve them both. When we turn in a later section to considering the effect of traditional norms on contemporary expectations this pattern will be seen to fit with certain aspects of Ibo and Ashanti kinship systems.

If the profile of scores for jointness of role structure is considered for the various activity spheres, as in Table 3.1, it is clear that the Ibo couples tend to be more joint than do the Ashanti. In constructing this profile, the scores for each activity sphere were divided into 'joint' and 'segregated' and a summary code compiled in which a couple was classified as either 'joint' or 'segregated' on each activity area. The total number of joint scores is twice as high for the Ibo couples (40 out of a possible 60 as compared to 19 out of a possible 60 for the Ashanti). For none of the individual activity spheres do Ashanti joint scores exceed, or even equal, those of the Ibo.

TABLE 3.1   *Comparison of jointness scores by activity sphere for Ibo and Ashanti*

	Ibo	Ashanti
Chores	3	2
Leisure	7	2
Finances	4	1
Decisions	9	4
Parental role	10	5
Communication	7	5
Total*	40	19

* Total possible score for each group is six activity spheres times ten couples = 60.

While comparison of Ashanti and Ibo profiles shows clearly that Ibo are more likely to structure marital roles jointly, there is a good deal of spread within each ethnic group. However, of the five couples who have clearly joint role patterns, four are Ibo; and of the seven for whom role segregation is very strong, six are Ashanti. In the following section we turn to consider the relationship between these 'jointness' scores and the level of stress observed in the household.

Indices of role stress within the marital family[6]

The lives of West Africans living, studying and working in London are very different from what they are accustomed to at home. Because of the fact that virtually all those who come here have attended secondary school or the equivalent, they represent a highly selected group. Two-thirds of the men had fathers who themselves went to school, while this must be true for a very small proportion indeed of the adult population of Ghana and Nigeria as a whole. Four-fifths of the fathers of the women in the sample had gone to school; they are an even more highly selected group. Economically they come from families of merchants, civil servants, clerks and professional men and they grew up in relative affluence, living in large houses, often with servants to see to the domestic chores and heavy work about the house and grounds.

In London none of the couples studied had any household help at all, and only three lived in a house by themselves. The most common pattern of accommodation is to rent two or three rooms and to have the use of a kitchen and bath which are often shared with other tenants. Rooms are small and shabby, and even for this meagre space the rent is usually high. Typically too, both husband and wife go out to work as well as taking full- or part-time courses of some kind. All the couples had children with them in England, though one couple sent their son home in the year of the study. The presence of children means not only cooking, washing and tidying up, and with babies constant feeding and changing of nappies, but it means also that arrangements must be made for someone to be with the children both in the day-time and at night. On top of the demands of jobs and studies, this requires considerable organisation, patience and determination to make a success of a difficult situation.

It is the context of both the taxing circumstances in London, and the contrast with what people have been used to at home, that the following indices of stress between husband and wife should be viewed. The ratings are grouped into six categories analogous to those used for the ratings of jointness of marital role. These categories are examined individually and then summary scores over the whole range of activities are outlined.

Domestic chores

As we have seen, in most couples, whether they are Ibo or Ashanti, the wife is responsible for the bulk of domestic chores despite the fact that she is usually working full-time. This being so, one might expect to find that domestic chores were a source of friction in many households, simply through the tiredness and lack of time on the wife's part. This does not in fact seem to be so, for over half of the couples are rated as showing low stress in this area. There is no real difference between Ibo and Ashanti in this respect. If, however, we look at the relationship between role segregation and stress, there does seem to be a pattern which holds for both groups. For it is those couples with joint responsibility for domestic chores who are most likely to be rated as low on stress over chores, and those couples who do not share domestic chores who are rated as showing moderate or high stress in this area. Here the sharing of chores is clearly more important in determining the ease of relations than the ethnic background of the couple.

Finances

Quarrels over money are a source of jokes about married life. If this is so in our society, it is even more likely to be the case when couples move into a highly monetised situation from one in which norms were to a large extent based on face-to-face relations with people in established relationships. 'In London everything is money.' Rent, electricity, food, clothes, car fares, school fees, entertainment, cigarettes, even the TV – all consume pennies and pounds at a steady pace. Of course with both husband and wife working, both have some income with which to meet these demands. But who should be responsible for which expenses? As outlined earlier, Ibo couples tend to decide jointly about major purchases, while this is less typical of the Ashanti. Most couples had arrived at a more or less tacit agreement about who should pay for what, wives generally buying the bulk of the food and clothes for small children, older girls, and themselves, while their husbands paid for the rent, utilities and clothes for the boys. But there was still room for disagreement. In the pattern of stress over day-to-day finances there is a difference between Ibo and Ashanti couples, with the former tending to have easy relations where finances are concerned while only three of the Ashanti couples were rated as showing no stress in this area. How does this index relate to the measure of role structure? The pattern is less clear than one would wish because there are so few couples in either group who structure financial roles jointly. However, all of those who do so fall into the 'low stress' cell while two-thirds of those whose financial roles are segregated were rated as showing 'high' or 'moderate' stress in this area. At the same time it is true that half of those rated as 'low stress' segregate their financial activities, so this is clearly not incompatible with an easy relationship.

Decision-making

A further question is whether the frequency of joint decision-making among Ibos was reflected in fewer stresses over decisions? While the same proportion of Ibo and Ashanti couples were rated as 'low' on stress over decisions, nearly all of the rest of the Ibo couples fell into the 'moderate stress' category, while the Ashanti were more likely to be rated as 'high stress'. There is a tendency, then, though no more than that, for Ashanti couples to show more stress about making decisions than the Ibo do. But what is the relationship between role structure and stress in respect to decision-making? The result suggests that there is some inverse relationship between jointness in decision-making and stress over the making of decisions. Those who make decisions independently nearly all show a high (as opposed to even a moderate) level of stress in this area, while nearly all those in the 'low stress' category follow a joint pattern of decision-making. It seems likely that the very process of having to make decisions is uncomfortable and tends to create some stress. This is the more probable when people are away from home and away from the counsel of kin and friends. But there seems to be something about the sharing of the decision-making process by husband and wife which reduces the strain associated with it. Or it may be that the greater strain apparent with couples among whom decisions are taken separately is due to added friction about the correctness of the decision itself. This was evident in some of the situations observed. Probably both factors are at work.

Leisure

Segregation of men's and women's activities is perhaps most apparent in the sphere of leisure since it would not seem to be imposed by external constraints such as work situation or physical character-istics. This pattern of segregation is still very evident among the Ashanti couples in London, but among the Ibo couples leisure activities are often pursued jointly. There appears to be a complete lack of correlation between the ethnic group of the sample couples and the incidence of stress over leisure activities. The same absence of correlation appears when role structure and degree of stress are considered together. Although it is of course possible that there is a real correlation here which has been masked by poor measures, it is equally likely that there are simply other factors which are more important than either norms derived from the ethnic group or *de facto* sharing of leisure pursuits. For instance it seemed in several cases that the jointness of leisure activities was related more closely to the age of children and whether the family had a car than to any other factors. But these constraints in turn will be perceived as deprivations or necessity depending on the expectations of the couple. For the present we must note that the problem of sharing of leisure and attitudes to this are complex, and not adequately handled by the simple measure offered above.

Parental role

In assessing the role structure of parental roles for Ibo and Ashanti it was found that all Ibo couples are at least moderately joint in this sphere. Ashanti couples, on the other hand, were distributed throughout the possible range of scores from highly joint to totally segregated in the way in which they carried out the role tasks. The same contrast appears in the pattern of stress ratings with respect to parental role behaviour for the two groups, but here all but one of the ten Ibo couples shows either moderate or high stress in relation to child-bearing. The Ashanti couples are again spread over the full range of scores, with over half rated as 'low' on stress in relation to parental roles. For Ashanti couples there is some tendency for jointness in parental role to be associated with low stress in this sphere, while couples with segregated parental roles tend to rate high on stress. This is the familiar pattern in other activity spheres. However for the Ibo couples the picture is very different. Despite the fact that all the couples were involved together in the joint rearing of their children, all but one were rated as showing either moderate or high stress in this area. Here the relation between jointness and low stress is reversed, and we find that for the strongly patrilineal Ibo, the sharing of parental responsibilities leads to considerable stress. The explanation is most likely to lie in the traditional structuring of parental and other roles, to be considered in a later section.

Communication and commitment

Although there was some tendency for the Ibo to define their roles more jointly (to plan more for a future together and to talk somewhat more freely), the relative level of stress over joint commitment for the two groups show no clear difference.[7] In both sub-samples there are couples who show little stress in interpersonal relations and seem well adapted to living together, and there are other couples who wage a constant struggle for dominance and avoid considering the future. But what happens when the form of role structure adopted by the couple is also taken into consideration? Here again we have a very clear association between jointly defined marital roles and low stress scores. Whereas stress in marital roles was not related directly to ethnic origin, it is related to whether the husband and wife structure their marital role jointly, whether they seem committed to a joint future and whether they communicate easily with one another.

A profile of stress scores by activity sphere for each of the two groups (using the frequency of moderate and high tension ratings), is a good basis for summarising the differences and similarities in the pattern of stress for the two groups.

In contrast to the summary table for role structure (Table 3.1), there is no difference between the Ibo and Ashanti couples in our sample in the overall levels of stress recorded in Table 3.2. Ashanti show more stress in certain areas – over domestic chores, financial arrangements, and very slightly more in commitment and communication. Ibo couples, on the other hand, show more stress in the remaining areas, particularly in respect of parental roles. The result is that the overall tension scores are identical for the two groups.

TABLE 3.2   *Comparison of stress scores by activity area for Ibo and Ashanti*

	Ibo	*Ashanti*
Chores	3	5
Leisure	6	5
Finances	3	7
Decisions	7	6
Parental role	9	4
Communication	7	8
*Total**	35	35

* Total possible score for each group is six activity spheres times ten couples = 60.

Relationships between marital role structure and role stress

In four of the six activity spheres – domestic chores, financial management, decision-making and communication – there seems to be a direct relationship between relatively low stress scores and jointly structured marital roles. This pattern appears very clearly in Table 3.3 where the scores of the twenty families on stress and role structure are summarised over these four activity spheres.

TABLE 3.3   *Relationship between role structure and stress scores[8] over four activity spheres*

		Role structure	
		Joint	Segregated
Stress	Low	33	10
	High	7	30

The association between joint marital roles and relatively low stress, and between segregated marital roles and relatively high stress must be explained. It is not a relationship that is obviously predictable for groups of this kind in which traditional marital roles are very highly segregated indeed. There seem to be three possible kinds of explanation, perhaps all of some merit.

First, at the level of interpersonal dynamics it is easy to see why the sharing of tasks and problems would lead to a greater appreciation by each spouse of the other's point of view, and thus to a greater tolerance.

Mr Akiga's shouldering of the running of the household during his wife's illness was associated with a high level of tolerance for her complaints and demands at the time. Since she has recovered and returned to work Peter Akiga continues to help so that they can both have free time at weekends. Perhaps more revealing, he supports Carol Akiga's wish to return to work, although he would prefer she didn't, because he says he realises what it is like for her cooped up in the house alone all day. (An Ibo case)

A more radical adaptation has occurred with the Ansahs, where Mr Ansah has pretty much taken over the household during the day so that his wife can go out to work. She only had part-time intermittent jobs while the children were very small, but now is determined to work full-time. Mr Ansah was at home for several weeks because of a strike, and took over the domestic chores so that his wife could work.

Now he has left work entirely and seems content to manage the household, while his wife is pleased to be able to hold a job. Of course, taking on of domestic tasks does not necessarily lead to such mutual adaptation. (An Ashanti case)

Mr Obemi's tolerance for domestic work apparently lasted only as long as his wife was obviously ill from overwork. Now that she is on her feet again he expects to be waited on as before. But this apparently deviant case is of some interest. For Mr Obemi is explicit in his view that men's and women's proper tasks are distinct and ought to be kept so. One of the advantages of life in Nigeria, he feels, is that people recognise this and don't expect men to do women's work. (An Ibo case)

This leads to the second of the explanations of the association between role segregation and relatively high levels of marital stress. Among the sample couples (as indeed elsewhere) stress was often expressed in the context of unfulfilled expectations.

Mrs Obemi, for instance, showed considerable frustration over her husband's failure to appreciate how hard she worked and his unwillingness to 'do his share'. This couple clearly have different ideas about what a husband's 'share' ought to be. Mrs Obemi's views are no doubt partly the result of the fact that she actually does work too hard (to the point where she became ill, and her friends were concerned) and that her husband did for a short time do quite a lot with the children and housework. Her hopes are also raised by the fact that at present Mr Obemi is working a night shift, so that he is about the house during the day and doing nothing at the same time that she is so much in need of help. (An Ibo case)

There is good reason to believe, however, that West Africans like those in this sample (who have read Western literature and magazines, and see newspaper and television reports) are considerably influenced by modern Western norms of the companionate marriage. It would seem probable that women are at least as susceptible to such ideas as men, if not more so since women have more to gain through the new norms. For according to these norms, women should share in decisions affecting the family while men should share in the chores, and both should spend free time together and have friends in common. The correspondence between these norms and joint marital role patterns is clear. Thus, particularly for women, the norm of joint marital role structure is likely to be a highly valued one. When the actual role structure is closer to the segregated model, then stress is likely to arise over this very discrepancy. To the extent that this explanation is correct, the association between segregated roles and a high level of marital stress is a product of the frustration of the new pattern of expectations of educated West African women; and the lower level of stress in couples whose marital roles are jointly structured reflects the fact that the new norms are shared and largely conformed to.

We have noted elsewhere (Goody and Muir, 1977) that the husband's studies are often made possible by the money his wife earns once she joins him in this country. This unaccustomed dependence on the wife would seem to be directly related to men's willingness to participate in domestic and child-care tasks. For West Africans living in the United Kingdom there is an immediacy to the symbiosis between husband and wife due to their isolation from other sources of support. Many husbands referred to the fact that their wives had helped them to study, and that it seemed only fair for them to lend a hand with the housework and children, so that the wife could take a job or study in her turn. And the complicated schedules which several couples had worked out to enable the wife both to work and to study while caring for the children testify to the efforts men are willing to make in this way.

The fond memories of 'doing everything together' recalled by women in West Africa who have spent some time in this country with their husbands would seem to be at least in part memories of the husband's willingness to come to his wife's assistance. In West Africa husbands are less likely to assist with domestic chores because there are alternative forms of assistance available. Many wives have younger kinswomen (either their own or their husband's) who live with the family, perhaps while attending school, and who carry the burden of domestic work. Others employ such a girl, often someone from a village, for whom a chance to live in the big city is deemed a great advantage. And professional households may have the services of a steward and a gardener, often as well as someone who comes in once or twice a week to do the washing and ironing. The contrast between the situation of the wife in West Africa and in London suggests a third explanation of the relationship between segregated marital roles and stress in marital relations. In West Africa the traditionally segregated roles of husband and wife may reduce the interests which they have in common with each other, but at the same time both men and women have various concerns in common with several other sets of people – kinsfolk often own farms or houses jointly, and may be in business together; men belong to clubs and societies like the Freemasons while women are involved in trading with other women, and often in church-based associations; men have colleagues at work, and both tend to have close friends from their school days. Interests and friendships outside the home balance the rather narrowly defined marital role. The picture in London is inevitably rather different, particularly for wives. Household and children fill most of the time available after work, and if she is studying as well, a woman has little time for meeting friends or joining interest groups or associations. Life becomes highly organised hard work, and free moments tend to be spent either sewing or sitting worn-out in front of the television. Some women have relatives who are also in the United Kingdom, and a few have close kin in London. Yet they have their own problems in combining work, study and family responsibilities and are seldom able to help. Hence the customary dependence on female kin for help in domestic tasks, and at times of extra stress such as illness and childbirth, is impossible. Both for leisure and for a helping hand, a wife turns to her husband far more than she must at home. Thus when a couple's role structure has not altered on coming to this country, but has remained segregated as in the traditional West African pattern, the wife is left without her usual compensatory associations.

The situation is less extreme for the husband for two reasons. In the first place, he does not have the responsibility of domestic arrangements and day-to-day chores as does his wife. The additional free time he thus gains is most often used for study, and most men are both working and studying for a further qualification of some kind. School, technical college or Inns of Court provide an additional set of contacts outside the home. Secondly, men can move more freely outside the home than can women. There are often parties at weekends, to celebrate a marriage, someone's completing his degree, an impending return home, or the arrival of a kinsman with news of relatives and townspeople. Men can go to such parties uninvited if they are acquainted with the host. But they do not bring their wives unless the couple have been specifically asked to attend. Apart from parties there are friends, pubs and 'business' as well as 'college', and many men seem to spend several evenings a week in one or another of these ways. Thus men are less vulnerable to isolation in London than are women, certainly less so than married women. It seems probable that the frustrations of this isolation are multiplied when few aspects of married life are in fact shared by the couple, and that it is in part as a result of this dual segregation that stress scores are so high for these couples.

Marital roles and the fostering of West African children in England

Among the nearly 300 couples interviewed in the survey during the first phase of the wider study, half either had children currently with English foster parents (25 per cent) or had previously fostered one or more children in this country (26 per cent). When we selected the twenty couples for intensive study, we planned to compare families where children had not been fostered with an equal number of those where they had. In fact we found later that one of the ten families selected as non-fostering had previously fostered a child, but the sample was roughly divided into four sets, consisting of Ashanti and Ibo couples who had fostered a child, and Ashanti and Ibo couples who had never done so. A central problem for the wider study was whether the fostering of children in this country was a response to situational contraints – the difficulty of both parents combining jobs and studies, poor housing, lack of resources for help in the home – or whether it was best understood as an adaptation of a traditional pattern of child-rearing to new circumstances. One dimension which we sought to examine was the effect of marital role structure and role stress on decisions to foster children in England. Ultimately this requires an examination of the fit between traditional and modern marital roles.[9]

For the purposes of this analysis the cases of fostering considered are those in which the child was actually sent to foster parents, and sent on the initiative of the parents themselves. (There were other instances in which the parents sought unsuccessfully to foster their children, and one case in which a social worker persuaded the reluctant couple to allow their son to be placed temporarily with foster parents.) Weekly minding arrangements have been treated here as fostering. They are very much midway between daily minding and fostering, but share with the latter the willingness of the parents to entrust a child to others for several days at a time.

Fostering is unusual for couples with decidedly joint marital role structure, while the majority of couples with highly segregated roles have fostered their children. Conversely, none of those with highly segregated marital role structure have cared for their children entirely on their own, although the majority of these with jointly structured roles do so. In order to meet the demands of both parents' jobs and studies a very high level of co-operation is necessary if young children are to be cared for in their own home. It is those couples who genuinely see the responsibilities involved as their joint concern who are able to sustain such an interdependence. For some of those couples where each is struggling for his or her own 'rights', children represent an added complication, and fostering a welcome situation. The wife in one couple, who had fostered their son once, brought him home, and then decided that he would be better off fostered again, said 'you see how he has crippled us'. With a relatively high degree of role segregation there was some co-operation in this family, but both husband and wife expressed resentment of the constraints their child's care placed on them, and of their dependence on the other to meet these.

No high stress couples are looking after their own children, and most of them have placed their children with foster parents. The few low stress couples show a preference for caring for their own children, but this is not clear-cut. Those whose relations are characterised by moderate stress are about equally likely to foster and to look after their children themselves. The interpretation of this material is made difficult by the feed-back effect of caring for children under the strenuous circumstances experienced by these couples. That is, couples whose children are being fostered are under less strain so far as tight schedules and domestic chores are concerned, than those with their children in the household.

It would appear that the expressions of role stress observed in these couples' behaviour are not directly related to the strains of managing children themselves. Of those looking after their children at the time of the study, only about one-quarter had high stress scores, while none of those whose children were currently fostered had low stress scores, and half of this group had high scores. The same pattern appears among those whose children are currently with daily minders; over half have high stress scores, and only one of the five in this category has a low stress score. No real confidence can be placed in such low numbers, but it does seem that the presence of children in the household is not itself responsible for high stress scores. If this is so then we appear to be justified in continuing to regard the indices of role stress as related to the several aspects of the marital relationship, and not simply to the immediate pressures of parenthood.

The clear finding from this material is that none of those parents who have chosen while in this country to care for their own children entirely have highly segregated marital roles, nor did any of them have high role stress scores. Those who do have highly segregated and relatively tense marital relations tend to foster their children. However the converse is not indicated: that is, fostering and daily minding are arranged by couples who do not have segregated and tense relations. Joint marital roles and a relatively stress-free relationship do not of themselves ensure that parents will decide against fostering and daily minding. This is not surprising in view of the many other factors important in decisions about child care. Crowded and substandard housing, the husband's determination to study as well as to support his family, and the wife's need to work and her attempts to train as well; all play their part, as does the concern to give the children an opportunity to learn English language and customs. As all these factors interact, it is difficult to assess their relative importance. It is also necessary to take into account the role of the cultural paradigm which defines the rearing of children outside the parental family as a valued form of education (Goody and Muir, 1977). Finally, the difference between Ibo and Ashanti traditions and social structures also plays a part in the way that couples in London perceive and respond to the constraints of living there.

Traditional matrilineal and patrilineal marital roles

Ibo

Any account of traditional social structure courts complaints of inaccuracy, since Ibo peoples occupy an area stretching from Benin to Igala, and from the Cross River to the Niger delta. Autonomous village clusters were the major form of settlement, and these recognised no central authority in pre-colonial times. While the Ibo peoples shared both language and culture, social organisation and traditions varied locally to some extent.[10] One of the most important single points in the present context is that the village clusters were made up of agnatic lineages (tracing descent through males) and were exogamous (marriages arranged with families living outside the village). Daughters were taught from early childhood that they would leave their own lineage village and marry permanently into another; at her marriage a woman joined the other wives of the lineage with whom she shared the role of valued stranger. The best way to establish a place for herself among her husband's people was to bear him sons who could continue the lineage and strengthen the village. As the mother of sons a woman was esteemed, and secure in her old age. Traditional Ibo marriage appears to have been very stable; that is, divorce was difficult, particularly for a woman to initiate, and seemingly rare. While a barren woman might return home to be replaced by a possibly more fertile sister, a mother had to leave behind her children. Thus even if she could persuade her brothers to refund her bridewealth, she had much to lose from leaving her husband. On the other hand, the wives of a village co-operated in trading and sometimes formed title associations within which a woman could win for herself a position of importance.

The Ibo wife was expected to assume responsibility for growing certain key foodstuffs, and thus for feeding her husband and children. Surplus food, salt and pottery could be traded at a slight profit which a woman was supposed to show her husband. Traditionally women were not allowed to trade for the first five years of their married lives, or when they had young children. Continuous trading activities were thus restricted to mature women, who could use the profits to help husbands and sons in their economic activities, or to buy titles. A barren wife could use her own resources to 'marry' a wife who would bear sons in her name to her husband. Trade took a woman to other nearby villages, but until the imposition of colonial rule, trips to other markets had to be made under the escort of men, for slave raiding and the seizing of women in retaliation for debts and wrongs were common. An Ibo woman was expected to work hard to feed her family and to trade for funds with which to advance them and herself. But her destiny was firmly bound up with that of her husband and her sons' future with his, and their lineage kin and resources.

Ashanti

Ashanti traditions and the structure of marital roles were forged initially during the growth of a kingdom of considerable power and wealth.[11] Although the army, and to some extent the judiciary, were focused on the capital at Kumasi, for many purposes the state was effectively decentralised in a number of divisions (*oman*), each of which had in turn a capital and usually also several important towns which owed allegiance to the divisional chief, as he (and they) did to the Asantihene. Thus Ashanti was a kingdom of dispersed towns linked by divisional and national loyalties. These loyalties were, however, mediated for the 'true' Ashanti by birthright in one of the localised lineages of the eight matrilineal clans found throughout the country. Every town contained several lineages of different clans, and thus although lineage exogamy (marrying out of the lineage) was the rule, most marriages could, and did, take place within the town. But not only was a woman usually able to remain in her natal village throughout her life; she very often remained in her own lineage compound as well. For having married in the same village as her husband, the couple were able to share the husband's room at night without either having to leave the companionship of their own lineage kin. The wife retained her room in her own compound (or shared her mother's or sister's) and co-operated with them still in farming and cooking, and later in the care of the children. One bowl of the food she cooked was sent to the husband's compound, where the men of his lineage could eat together, while the wife and her children ate with the other women and children of her lineage. As they grew more independent, sons tended to spend increasing amounts of time with the father in his compound, and often slept in his room. The father had two main responsibilities in the rearing of his sons: he should teach them whatever economically important skills he knew (for example, the working of gold or weaving and carpentry), and he should see that they knew the Ashanti morality. But father and son knew that ultimately, on the father's death if not before, the son would return to live in the compound of his maternal kin, to come directly under the authority of the head of his matrilineage segment, a 'grandfather' or a 'mother's brother'. For it was within this segment that the son's rights of inheritance lay, and only by virtue of his membership of his maternal lineage that he could be a useful citizen of the town, and perhaps one day hold office.

Divorce in Ashanti was a relatively simple matter, partly because there was no bridewealth to be refunded, and partly because the wife was usually already living most of the time with her own people. Even if she was not, it was easy to move her things into a room in her maternal compound and take up formal residence there. Even those women who went through life with a single husband, and who lived with him in his own compound, tended to return to their matrilineage compound once their children were grown. For their children's future was anchored there, and thus their own as well. In old age a woman in her own lineage compound is the focus of the women's courtyard, receiving greetings and organising the work of the household. As her daughters grow and marry, her grandchildren join the group, and she sees the succeeding generations of her lineage develop under her guidance. Marriage for an Ashanti woman was important for many reasons, not the least of which was the desire to have legitimate children with a father who would guide and train them. But its persistence was not necessary to secure her own or the children's future.

The Ashanti wife was expected to cultivate a farm in which the basic vegetable foodstuffs were grown. She was thus responsible for the provision of the staples on which she and her husband and children depended. A good husband provided meat or fish for the soup, but a wise woman learned how to make soups of leaves, peppers, okra and tomato that was palatable without protein. If a woman left her husband, or if when he died she preferred not to marry one of his 'brothers', then the men of her lineage would assume the responsibility of providing her with land for a farm, and clearing it of the heavy forest ready for cultivation. Because of this a woman was able to support herself and her children whether or not she had a husband to provide for her. Petty trading with surplus foodstuffs, or with trade goods bought in the larger towns provided small sums for cloth and cosmetics, while her brothers and the senior members of the lineage segment were ready to help and advise in case of illness or trouble, for she was not only their sister, but also the mother of the lineage heirs.

Each of these two societies is, of course, unique in many ways. However, each also shares several key features with other matrilineal and patrilineal groups, though certainly not with all. But in transmission of land rights, and rights to other major resources, in eligibility to positions of ritual and political authority, and, of course, in the principle of recruitment to corporate kin groups, the Ibo are typically patrilineal and the Ashanti representative of matrilineal systems. To this limited extent, then, the general points made for these two systems can be treated as hypotheses which are worth testing for other patrilineal and matrilineal West African societies.

Relationships between traditional and contemporary marital roles among Ibo and Ashanti in London

If the scores for marital role structure and stress for the Ibo and Ashanti families in our intensive sample are plotted on a scatter diagram (Figure 3.1) the broad association between segregated role structure and high stress scores already noted is clear. Even more striking, however, is the lack of overlap between the scores of the two groups. The Ashanti cases fall into two quite separate clusters, one low on stress and with relatively joint role structure, and the other high on stress with segregated marital roles. The Ibo pattern, on the other hand, is rather different, with most couples falling in the relatively joint end of the role structure scale, but showing a wide range of stress scores. To put this in another way, although for each group joint role structure is associated with the lower stress scores, of the six couples in each group with relatively high stress scores, five Ashanti couples but only one Ibo couple have strongly segregated roles. Thus Ibo as a group have less segregated marital roles, while only two of the ten Ashanti couples were classified as clearly joint.

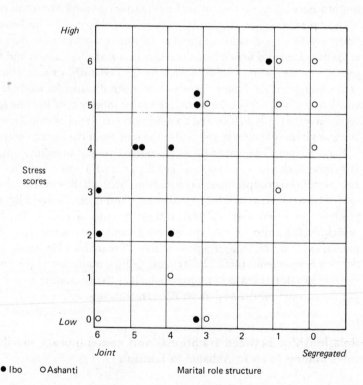

FIGURE 3.1   *Scatter diagram showing relation between role structure and role stress scores for Ibo and Ashanti couples*

This pattern of relatively joint roles among Ibo couples, and of the relatively segregated role structure of Ashanti couples in our sample can be seen to fit with the traditional marital roles of both groups. The interests of the traditional Ibo wife were strongly identified with those of her husband, as was the future of her sons. In working for herself she worked for her husband, his brothers and their sons, to feed them and to help them better their status in the community. The new norms of Christianity and Western liberalism, stressing the importance of monogamy, represent for the Ibo wife a welcome acknowledgement of the investment she has made in her marriage, and we venture to suggest that monogamy is the more acceptable to Ibo men because of their wives' clear commitment. One index of this in the Ibo families of our sample is the fact that all of them had been married, by Church and civil law, that is, in a form which requires monogamy and makes divorce complicated and difficult. In this they contrast strongly with the Ashanti couples, half of whom had been married by customary rites only. This reluctance of Ashanti couples to enter into a formal commitment to marriage as a permanent tie is reflected in our assessment of the degree of *de facto* commitment to their marriages. For six out of the ten couples we rated this as 'low', while with the Ibo couples there was only one such 'low' rating. While it might be argued that the decision to marry in a form legally binding in Western law was related more directly to church membership than anything else, this does not fit our observations. The majority of the sample, including the majority of the Ibo, are not actively religious. Indeed some Ibo reported that the events of the Biafran war had finally persuaded them of the emptiness of church doctrine. On the other hand, while all of the Ashanti women, and nearly all of the men, classified themselves as belonging to one or another Christian denomination, in this case this does not lead regularly to a church or civil marriage.

The suggestion is that Ibo couples in London are likely to have relatively joint marital roles because they are both committed to their marriage, and both are ready to see chores and problems as concerning them equally. While traditional Ibo roles of husband and wife differentiated clearly between men's and women's tasks, their *goals* were common. Joint efforts contributed to joint achievement. The situation in London is very similar to this. Both must work hard to enable the husband to fulfil his ambitions and support the growing family both desire. The husband recognises the importance of his wife's contribution, and is often willing to make sacrifices in order that she too can manage to fulfil her ambitions for learning new skills. It is often accepted by both that the wife's skills will ultimately be employed in a job, or in her own business, in such a way as to benefit them and their children, as well as enabling them to meet obligations to kin.

The situation of Ashanti couples in London proves to be quite different. Half are married by customary law only, and several have left children at home in Ghana, usually with the wife's mother. Only two have more than a single child with them in this country, and one couple has sent both their children home. They tend to live as one-child families, and this despite the fact that the length of time spent in this country is very similar for the two groups. Overtly, the Ashanti wives' pattern of work does not differ from that of the Ibo women. But while the Ibo women spoke of the responsibility to contribute to the expenses of the household, the Ashanti wives tended to be more concerned about retaining some degree of control over the support of the family in case they should have to manage on their own. Plans for the future tended to take the same form. Thus, when Mrs Kyei spent her weekends styling hair and setting wigs after a full week's factory work, it was not because she needed the extra money for current expenses but because she was determined to buy as much equipment as possible for a hairdressing salon she intended to establish at home. This she must do, she said, in order to be sure of the future, for her marriage was not going well and it was likely that she would have to fend for herself. In the course of contacting couples for the intensive study, we encountered several Ashanti women who had been married here, but were now in England on their own, sometimes with children, and trying to complete training which would enable them to be independent on their return.

In many ways this too represents a continuity with traditional marriage patterns, for it seems that divorce was fairly common in Ashanti. The difference, of course, is that a woman who married in her own town could easily go home to mother and brothers, and the lineage resources were there to look after her. When a woman in London or Accra finds that her marriage has broken down, she is in a much more difficult situation. It is probably still true that she could go home to her own room in the maternal home, but brothers may no longer live there together, at hand to support their maternal kin, and if she has been to school and started to work she may no longer be content to farm and trade for a modest livelihood. For those from a matrilineal background like Ashanti, modern urban life has in effect exaggerated the separateness of men's and women's destinies. Their degree of commitment to marriage may be relatively low (as it proved to be in our sample couples), perhaps in part because in their experience marriage is an institution which pertains to only *some* of the important concerns and activities of adult life. The numbers committed to marriage in traditional Ashanti could not be very high because of the strong claims made by the matrilineage on the children, and on the parents themselves in their alternative roles as brother and mother's brother, sister and grandmother. But whereas the matrilineage was formerly there to provide support and a focus for achievement and loyalty, this is no longer the case. Thus the individual must be prepared to manage on his or her own, and for women this throws into relief the need to be able to support themselves.

It seems that the Ashanti couples in our sample have relatively segregated marital roles, in part at least, because although they are mutually dependent on each other at the present time, they have difficulty in seeing themselves as equally closely interdependent in the future. When this situation of anticipated disengagement coincides with the customary rather rigid segregation of roles along sex lines, experience easily appears to confirm these fears. For instance, it is common for West African men to continue to go to parties alone even after they marry, and many men in the sample couples were out several nights a week on social or business affairs. While some Ibo wives resent this, others see it as 'the way men are'. But such behaviour did not appear to be threatening any of the marriages of the Ibo couples. Ashanti wives, on the other hand, are apt to see this as evidence that the husband has lost interest and may be forming another serious relationship.

In short, it seems that the stable marriage and common goals of the traditional Ibo family have evolved into relatively stable marriages with a high level of commitment to a joint future, and that this is associated with the sharing of chores and decision-making and a certain number of common leisure pursuits, that is, with joint marital roles. Conversely, the Ashanti tradition of loyalties and responsibilities divided between the matrilineage and the marital family has set up a pattern of opposition between the interests of husband and wife which tends to be expressed in modern conditions in relatively segregated marital roles, a continued low level of commitment to the marital union, and probably to relatively high divorce. It is interesting to note that the traditional Ashanti pattern of parenthood which sees this as persisting independently of the fate of the parents' marriage seems to make it easier for Ashanti parents to agree about their children's upbringing.

4

This paper considers the psychological process of identity development among adolescents. The comparative perspective of this paper reminds us that we are all subject to the same psychological pressures which produce our changing self-concepts but it indicates also that there are special pressures faced by children of ethnic minorities. These differences result from their position in the wider society and not, as it is often assumed, from problems inherent in the minority populations.

This is a clear exposition of the constructive potential of stress. The paper argues that conflicts in, or alternatives of, identification are valuable and normal resources, not the peculiar liabilities of immigrant children. While the results of the research show that minority adolescents have a higher incidence of identification conflict with people of their own ethnic category than white adolescents do, they do not support the idea that this inevitably leads to a devaluation of self.

Ethnicity and Adolescent Identity Conflicts

A comparative study

Peter Weinreich

All adolescents go through a process of identity development during which they change their images of themselves. They need to feel that they are not simply extensions of their parents, but that they are separate individuals. They experiment with various roles, try them on for fit, reject some components and accept others. They formulate their own points of view on a range of topics, such as dress, music, boy and girl friends, and begin to scrutinise given moral imperatives. Adolescents of Asian or Caribbean descent who identify primarily with their parents' culture will behave differently from those who identify more with various indigenous groupings such as native white boys and girls at school, their teachers, or heroes from the predominantly white mass media. If they forge a conception of themselves which is neither approved by their parents, nor by their native white peers they may find that they have to withstand considerable psychological conflict.

This paper[1] has three basic aims. First, it outlines an approach to identity development which regards an individual's conflicts in identification with others as being an important psychological impetus for personal change. In this view 'identity conflict' is regarded as being more frequently a resource than a liability. Secondly, it reports the findings of a study on patterns of ethnic identification conflicts in a sample of Bristol, England, school-leavers consisting of boys and girls of Asian, Caribbean and native white parentage. The results demonstrate that ethnic identity conflicts do not generally imply self-hatred which is so often assumed. And thirdly, the paper draws tentative conclusions about possible ethnic identity developments in these Bristol adolescents. Clear differences are noted between Asians and West Indians, and between West Indian boys and girls.

Definitions of identification

Erik Erikson (1959, 1968) postulates that identity formation involves a synthesis of the prior identifications which the person has formed with various significant people during his or her socialisation. The synthesising process cannot, however, be equated with a simple amalgamation. If it were, there would be no conceptual problem. It is something more complex, and it is necessary to take into account that many of a person's identifications will be incompatible with one another. The thesis presented here is that change and development in people's identities come about as the result of their conflicts in identifications with others. It argues that, *through their attempts to resolve identification conflicts*, people change their self-concepts.

In wishing to explain how 'identity is synthesised' it is necessary to query how identification conflicts become established and how they become resolved. With our concern here for processes of *ethnic* identity development the question becomes one of finding out how ethnicity is related to the establishment of identification conflicts. Deductions may then be drawn about the way in which identity development will proceed among adolescents of different ethnic backgrounds.

Before turning to the results of the empirical study, we have to examine more fully what we mean by a person's conflict in identification with another and indicate how such conflicts may be empirically measured. This in turn requires a clarification of the term 'identification', two distinct senses of which can be distinguished. It may refer to a person's wish to become like another whom he or she admires, or it may denote a person's recognition of sameness with another. In the first sense the other represents qualities which have become incorporated into the person's ideal self-image, whilst in the second he or she recognises that the other shares the *same* qualities, good or bad, with his or her own experienced self. This conceptual distinction is important in arriving at a definition of a person's identification conflict with another: the two senses will therefore be defined separately. Identifications with others are generally partial and not absolute. People do not identify in an all or none fashion with the values and characteristics of various groups and individuals. They usually identify with some and dissociate from others, forming several part identifications with other people. The following definitions therefore include statements about the extent of a person's identification with another.

A definition of identification in terms of *perceived similarity* is straightforward. With a person's current self-image as reference point:

> the extent of a person's *current identification* with another is defined as the degree of similarity between the qualities he or she attributes to the other (whether 'good' or 'bad') and those of his or her current self-image (me as I am now).

The other use of the concept refers to people's ideal self-images and relates to their reference models or groups either as ones whom they wish to emulate, or as ones forming contrasting standards for comparison. Two definitions follow corresponding to the distinction between emulation and contrasting standards:

> the extent of a person's *idealistic-identification* with another is defined as the degree of similarity between the qualities he or she attributes to the other and those he or she would like to possess as part of an ideal self-image (me as I would like to be).

> the extent of a person's *contra-identification* with another is defined as the degree of similarity between the qualities he or she attributes to the other and those from which he or she would wish to dissociate.

People's idealistic-identifications constitute their positive value systems associated with their more positive reference models, whilst their contra-identifications are linked with their contra-value systems and their more negative reference models.

In general, therefore, a person's current identifications will be spread across a number of significant others. If he currently identifies with someone in whom he perceives characteristics from which he wishes to dissociate, his identification with that other will be conflicted. An interesting example occurs in a West Indian girl who was a respondent in the study reported in these pages. Her identification with a group of Pakistani girls was conflicted. She perceived herself as currently sharing several characteristics with them, mostly good ones but some bad (for instance, those which she appreciated in herself and in them included an inner strength, an interest in the personality of members of the opposite sex, moderation in aggressive behaviour, a belief in free choice in marriage, a lack of meanness with money, sincerity, etc.; those which she would rather not have seen in herself, but which she shared with them included a lack of confidence, a dependence on others, unassertiveness, a lack of wit, etc.). Thus, in terms of the definitions given above, the extent of her *current identification* with them was high.

She perceived this group of girls not only as having some unwelcome characteristics in common with herself, but also as having additional ones not in common ('they keep to themselves', 'they find it hard to get a job', etc.). All these together contributed to the overall extent of her *contra-identification* with Pakistani girls according to the definition given above. Her current self-concept therefore included a component made up of her partial, but simultaneously occurring current- and contra-identifications with Pakistani girls, that is, a specific conflict in identification with them of a certain magnitude. It also included, of course, a number of other identification conflicts dispersed across other individuals and groups of people.

In the normal course of events a person has various levels of conflicts in identification with different others. The concept of a person's *conflict in identification with another* replaces the loose and ambiguous term 'identity conflict'.[2] Whereas 'identity conflict' could be used to refer only to some general notion of conflict associated with a person's self-concept, a person's conflicts in identifications can be located precisely in relation to particular individuals and groups. This is a feature of considerable importance in investigating differences between ethnic groups, because it becomes possible thereby to examine adolescents' identification conflicts with respect to representatives of different ethnicities. It enables a shift to be made from the generality of unspecified 'identity conflict' to specific 'identification conflicts' with particular others. In so far as the term 'identity conflict' retains any utility it is in the restricted and non-specific sense of referring to large and dispersed conflicted identifications within a person's self-concept. As such its ambiguity is evident as it can refer to many different kinds of distribution of specific identification conflicts with all kinds of individuals and groups.

The translation of these concepts into empirical quantitative measures depends on a technique which uses Kelly's theory of personal constructs (Kelly, 1955; Bannister and Mair, 1968; Bannister and Fransella, 1972). Each individual has a finite number of bipolar constructs by means of which he is able to construe others, that is, to judge and to differentiate between them on a number of personally relevant dimensions. A person's construct system incorporates his values. The approach can therefore be used with adolescents from different cultural backgrounds without violating their differing value systems and world-views. It is equally applicable to any language or dialect (Weinreich, 1975a).

The study

Ethnic identification conflicts were studied in a sample of adolescent boys and girls of native white, Asian and Caribbean parentage respectively. They were Bristol school-leavers randomly selected at a low frequency from a number of schools, with a control for comparable classroom experience. Their ages at first contact were fifteen to sixteen years. In practice, all Asian boys and girls in the school-leaving year were included because of their low concentration in Bristol schools. There were thirteen Asian, thirty-two West Indian, and thirty-seven white adolescents in the sample.[3] Their constructs were elicited during semi-structured probing interviews which ranged across various areas of life experience – for example family, schools, friends, outstanding childhood events, anticipations of the future, feelings about society, their own and other people's characteristics, etc. Notes were made of all significant others mentioned. They were then presented, individually, with their own constructs and asked to construe systematically, using rating scales, their significant others and their own self-images. These individual but controlled construals provided the basic data for the analysis of each person's conflicts in identifications with others.

The adolescents' positive value systems are determined by reference to their construals of their ideal self-images, positive values being aligned with how they would ideally like to be. Their contra-value systems are assumed to be aligned with the contrasts associated with their underlying bipolar constructs (for example, 'believes in law and order', contrast: 'each man for himself'; 'studies for something worthwhile', contrast: 'works just for the money', etc.). Each adolescent is thereby viewed as having construed others and his or her current self-image in terms of characteristics which have specific value connotations which are peculiar to him- or herself. Their construals of their current self-images and their significant others are compared to determine their degrees of current-identifications with them. Their contra-identifications with others are calculated as the extents to which they attribute characteristics to them which reflect their contra-value systems. Their conflicts in identifications with others can then be assessed by taking the product of the individual's simultaneous current- and contra-identifications with each significant other in turn.

Analysis and results

Respondents were able to construe a full range of their significant others. But for the purposes of this analysis attention was restricted to ethnically related targets of their construals, that is, general representatives of ethnic groups (e.g. Jamaican adults, Jamaican boys, English girls, Pakistanis, etc.) and their own parents. Other members of their families were excluded because differences in family size could bias the results, as when one person has five siblings and another none with whom he might have identification conflicts. Only the presence or absence of a person's identification conflicts with people coming under four headings – parents, own ethnic group, other ethnic group 1, other ethnic group 2 – were recorded: double, treble or more items under one heading were treated simply as indicating the presence of conflict. This tabulation showed for each person whether his highest identification conflicts clustered around his own ethnic group, his parents, some other ethnic group, or any combination of these.

The aggregate results are presented in Table 4.1, which gives the distribution of ethnically related high identification conflicts for the Bristol sample. Reading across for English boys, 47 per cent (7 out of 15) have some of their high identification conflicts with their parents and the same percentage with other general categories of native whites. Sixty per cent and 40 per cent of them have similarly high conflicts in identification with general categories of people fitting the umbrella terms 'West Indian' and 'Asian' respectively.

The data point to some striking and important differences between the adolescents of the three ethnic groups. English boys and girls do not display any specific concentration of high identification conflicts with parents or with representatives of the three ethnic groups. (Using the incidence with their own ethnic group as a base line for comparison, no statistically significant deviations are found in incidence with parents, West Indians and Asians.)

TABLE 4.1 *Distribution of high identification conflicts by ethnicity and sex*

% of such conflicts present (% present + % absent = 100%) in relation to:

(N)		Parents	Own ethnic group	West Indians	Asians
(15)	English boys	47	47	60	40
(22)	English girls	32	55	59	45
(37)	Together	38	51	60	43

(N)		Parents	Own ethnic group	English	West Indians
(7)	Asian boys	14	100	57	43
(6)	Asian girls	17	83	50	83
(13)	Together	15^L	92^{HH}	54	61

(N)		Parents	Own ethnic group	English	Asians
(14)	West Indian boys	21^L	79^{HH}	86^{HH}	29^L
(18)	West Indian girls	55^H	95^{HH}	39^L	28^L
(32)	Together	41	87	59	28

NOTE   Chief characteristics which differentiate the groups at a statistically significant level: HH = high presence; H = moderately high; L = low.
Reading across L v HH, p< 0.001; H v HH; p < 0.01.
Reading down (West Indian boys and girls) L v HH; p < 0.01; L v H, p = 0.055.

The thirteen Asian boys and girls, although a small number, show a high degree of consistency. They manifest a very high proportion of incidence of identification conflicts (92 per cent) with general representatives of their own ethnicity, contrasted with a very low proportion with their own parents (15 per cent) (a difference significant at beyond the 0.1 per cent probability level using the Fisher exact probability test of statistical significance).

Significant differences separate out West Indian boys from girls. Both boys and girls have very high incidences of identification conflicts with their own ethnic group – in this, they resemble the Asian boys and girls. But the boys differ from the girls in two important respects: first, a very high proportion of them have high levels of identification conflicts with the English whilst only a low proportion of girls do (a difference significant at the 1 per cent level); and second, their incidence with their own parents is low compared with the moderately high incidence found in the girls (a difference arising with a probability by chance of 5.5 per cent only) (see Driver, this volume). We therefore have to consider the distributions of ethnic identification conflicts for West Indian boys and girls separately.

The pattern for the boys consists of a high proportion of identification conflicts with their own ethnicity and with the English, but not with their own parents nor with Asians (these differences are significant at beyond the 0.1 per cent level). The girls, by contrast, have a low incidence with the English, but a moderately high incidence with their own parents (comparing these with the high proportion of identification conflicts with their own ethnicity, they differ at levels significant at 0.1 per cent and 1 per cent respectively).

Discussion

A common feature of both minority group adolescents is their high incidence of identification conflicts with people of their own ethnicity – in absolute terms *and* compared with whites. About 90 per cent of the boys and girls of immigrant parentage (whether Asian or Caribbean) manifest such conflicts compared with about 50 per cent of indigenous white boys and girls. What can account for the fact that, despite other differences in their patterns of ethnic identification conflicts, Asian and West Indian adolescents consistently have conflicted identifications with their primary ethnic groups?

The most probable explanation is that their socialisation experiences have involved two cultures, in which one – their parents' – is in a primary but subordinate relationship to the other – that of the indigenous population. All of these adolescents have experienced early socialisation within the minority culture of their parents, followed by increasing exposure to socialisation within the majority culture represented by formal education in primary and/or secondary schools and by the mass media (of the forty-five immigrant boys and girls in the sample, seven had had all their primary and secondary education, and a further twenty-six had had part of their primary and all their secondary education in England). This means that their primary allegiances are first grounded in their own ethnic groups. But their subsequent socialisation presents alternative views which, when they are in part adopted, conflict with their earlier identifications with their own ethnicity. Hence, despite other differences between the minority groups, conflicts in identification with people of their own ethnicity will tend to prevail for them all.

An alternative explanation would argue that their identity conflicts are the manifestation of their plight in a discriminatory society. According to this interpretation black and brown children would internalise the derogatory view of their own ethnic groups held by the majority whites and form devalued self-images.[4] Their identity conflicts would be based in their self-rejection or self-hate and their identification with the aggressor, that is, white people. Despite the currency of this kind of explanation in academic and psychiatric literature, its validity is doubtful, except in a minority of individual cases. It receives no support as a generalisation from the present study. The evidence demonstrates that there is no substantial difference between the adolescents of Caribbean parentage and indigenous whites in their mean evaluations of adults, and boys and girls of their own ethnicity (Table 4.2).

TABLE 4.2   *Evaluation of own ethnic group*

Evaluation: range − 1.00 to + 1.00

	(N) Adults	(N) Own sex peers	(N) Opposite sex peers
English boys	(12) 0.58	(13) 0.53	(13) 0.49
English girls	(14) 0.35	(16) 0.40	(16) 0.27
West Indian boys	(13) 0.47	(12) 0.44	(14) 0.43
West Indian girls	(17) 0.28	(16) 0.33	(18) 0.17

Analysis of variance: (i) no significant ethnic difference in evaluation of own group members, whether adults, own or opposite sex peers; (ii) girls have a significantly lower evaluation than boys do of adults, own and opposite sex peers of their own ethnicity ($p < 0.01$).

NOTE   Variation in Ns arises from the idiographic approach to the study in which the significant others for each respondent varied, so that respondents would not always have identical target groups to evaluate.

To the extent that they have a somewhat lower evaluation of their own peoples than whites have of theirs, the amount is small compared with a large sex difference. Irrespective of ethnicity, it is girls compared with boys who have a low opinion of adults, the opposite sex and even their own sex. The minority adolescents' slightly lower evaluation of their own group does not amount to a general internalisation of a derogatory view. There is no evidence that they generally devalue themselves compared with whites. Table 4.3 presents data which suggest that, if anything, the immigrant adolescents tend to have higher self-esteem than whites. (All the measures of evaluation are based on each person's individual value system, i.e. his own way of evaluating the social world as opposed to 'standard' scales which impose the investigators' values on the respondents.)

TABLE 4.3   *Self-esteem by ethnicity – boys and girls combined**
Self-esteem: range −1.000 to +1.000

	(N) English	(N) West Indian and Asian		
Including cases of 'defensive high self-esteem'	(37) 0.375†	(45) 0.512†	(32) 0.475 West Indian	(13) 0.605 Asian
Excluding cases of 'defensive high self-esteem'‡	(37) 0.375	(39) 0.470	(28) 0.434 West Indian	(11) 0.563 Asian

* Analysis of variance indicates no significant gender differences in self-esteem.
† The difference between these means is significant at $p < 0.05$ (analysis of variance).
‡ Four West Indian and two Asian adolescents are identified as exhibiting 'defensive high self-esteem'.

These findings – that minority adolescents have identification conflicts centred on their own ethnicity, and that this is usual and does not indicate pathological self-hatred – are in line with conclusions drawn by Parker and Kleiner (1966). These authors report a major study of mental illness in urban blacks in the United States in which psychiatric patients were compared with a non-psychiatric community sample. They conclude that:

Although ambivalence in identification patterns has often been associated with psychopathology in the clinical literature ambivalence in the present instance may well be realistic and adaptive for the Negro. It is the polarization of racial identification or reference group behaviour that is psychopathogenic. Our data show that the psychiatrically healthy Negro is an individual with conflicts about his racial identification.

Identity development

The results of this study may be used to make tentative predictions about the different ways in which these adolescents' self-concepts are likely to develop. This exercise can be no more than illustrative of the different kinds of developments which may be observed in adolescents of West Indian and Asian parentage. The frequencies of occurrence in the population at large can only be uncertain, given that the empirical work is restricted to Bristol. However, the importance of these predictions is that they demonstrate the inevitability of social change through the dynamics of self-concept change, and that the changes themselves may be other than those expected by various sections of the different communities.

The predictions are based on the thesis that people, in trying to resolve their identification conflicts, will change their self-concepts. Elimination of such conflicts is not expected, only that the direction of self-concept change will be in line with partial resolutions of the person's major ones. It is probable that new ones will become established as people continue to interact with others whose self-concepts also change, and as they form new identifications with others whom they meet for the first time in a variety of settings.

The definition of a person's identification conflict with another indicates the ways by which he may strive to resolve that conflict. Being a multiplicative function of the extents of his simultaneous current- and contra-identifications with the other, his conflicted identification would decrease in magnitude if he could diminish *either* his current- *or* his contra-identification with that other.

A diminution in his current identification amounts to a lessening of the similarity of the other to himself, that is, marking the other off by distinction. For example, not only is the other different in his skin colour as previously observed, but he is reappraised as being also overbearing, rude and abusive of his power. In other words, if the person retains his own value-system intact, this process involves him in re-appraising the characteristics of the other in such a way as to emphasise the other's dissimilarity to himself. If he does this by attributing further characteristics to the other from which he would wish to dissociate, as in the example, he will evaluate the other more unfavourably than before. However, actual changes in his *own* self-concept would be restricted to possible re-evaluations of himself in terms of his existing value system; for example, he may see himself as being more competent than before at certain tasks when 'competence' is one of his continuing values.

In the second process the individual would strive to decrease his contra-identification with the other. He could do this in two ways. One would be by reappraising the other in a favourable direction by reference to his existing value system, which he could do only if the other were already seen to be changing in the direction of his positive values. The second would be by his restructuring his value system so that he came to interpret as favourable those characteristics in the other he formerly perceived as being undesirable. An example would be when a person had formerly interpreted another's verbal expressions as being aggressive, but then reformulates his own values so that he comes to reinterpret the same verbal behaviour as being assertive. In this case the individual would have restructured the *criteria* for his own self-construal as well as for the other. The latter process is one that entails *qualitative* changes in people's self-construals. These are more profound in their implications for social change than are the other ways of diminishing identification conflicts, which may possibly involve changes in self-evaluation, but only in terms of people's existing value-systems.

The analysis of projected self-concept change in the Bristol sample of adolescents will assume that most of them will attempt the last mentioned restructurings of self-concepts at least to some degree. Given the limited interest of the other processes to changes of substance, the predictions that follow will be restricted to this analysis alone (the other processes are however of importance when considering certain dynamics in the generation of hostility towards others, and in the acquisition of self-esteem).

Asian boys and girls

The results of the Bristol study indicate that school-leaving Asian boys and girls have conflicted identifications with general representatives of their own ethnic group, but not, significantly, with their own parents. This suggests that a common theme in their future identity development will be the reappraisal of their own ethnicity. But owing to their non-conflictual identifications with their parents, their continuing allegiance to their ethnic group is in most cases assured – few are likely to reject their ethnic roots.

Whilst redefining their ethnicity towards a radically modernised view of 'Asian-ness', most of them will retain an ethnically distinctive life-style. These Asian adolescents are likely to question the current norms within their own community and redefine what being a young Asian man or woman in Britain should entail (see C. Ballard, this volume). The participation of Asian women in work situations and the increasing say that young people have in choosing marriage partners, indicate the kinds of changes that support this interpretation. In this process, however, their distinctiveness as Asians is not undermined. Their religious and moral values retain a cohesiveness which stems from the young people's acceptance of their parents' influence in their identity formation.

The retention of their ethnic distinctiveness will mean that they are likely to continue to remain apart from native whites and, in this sense, not assimilate to them. But their redefinitions of themselves will involve an adaptation to, and incorporation of, some of the cultural values of the native white institutions.

West Indian boys and girls

Although there were relatively few boys and girls of Asian parentage in the Bristol sample, they were remarkably homogeneous with respect to the ethnic locus of their identification conflicts. This was not true for the adolescents of Caribbean parentage. The patterns of ethnic identification conflicts in the girls differed from those in the boys. We should therefore expect self-concept changes to differ across the sexes (see Driver, this volume).

As an aggregate, the West Indian boys have conflicted identifications with general representatives of both their own ethnicity and the native white population. This implies that individual boys will work towards resolving their identification conflicts in a variety of ways. Differing emerging self-definitions should be expected, though two broad orientations may be anticipated. These will depend on whether the boys will work primarily towards resolving their identification conflicts with native whites, or with their own ethnicity.

In attempting to resolve their identification conflicts with respect to their own ethnicity, some will work towards a more consciously defined ethnic conception based upon an internal restructuring of their value systems. In the process they may partially resolve their conflicted identifications with native whites by increasingly dissociating from them. Such an orientation would lead to an emphasis on their ethnic distinctiveness, with, for example, an increasing concern with the hallmarks of their ethnicity in terms of their ancestral roots. Some may increasingly define themselves in terms of the particular part of the Caribbean from which their parents come. Others may go further and imbue their self-concepts with core ideas of African ancestry. Different ramifications would follow from these kinds of developments. Those who increasingly define their roots in an African ancestry will tend to identify more strongly than others with political movements in Africa which aim to free indigenous cultures from alien colonial and neo-colonial influences. Those who look to the Caribbean for their roots are more likely to be concerned with political and social developments there. In both cases, however, an important part of their ethnic allegiance will be towards their roots and, to that extent, outwards from Britain.

Other West Indian boys may attempt to resolve their identification conflicts with native whites by an internal restructuring of their values towards a closer identification with them. In some cases this would be accompanied by a partial resolution of their conflicted identifications with certain sections of their own group through an increasing dissociation from them. Some may try to adopt a blind eye to skin-colour differences and to define themselves as British, say, particularly as Bristolians, and speak with an appropriate accent and share the local folklore. In the present climate of prejudice people with such self-definitions are likely to deny, or to play down, discrimination against them. If their psychological orientations become those of generalised defensive denial, their identity developments may be arrested for a time in states known as foreclosed identities (Hauser, 1971; Erikson, 1959). The latter may include cases of 'defensive high self-esteem', that is people who manifest high levels of self-esteem which are accompanied by unusually low degrees of identification conflicts, indicating a reluctance to acknowledge such conflicts. (Note: No suggestion is being made that minority individuals with high self-esteem are generally exhibiting 'defensive denial'. High self-esteem will mostly signify realistic adaptations and recognition of identification conflicts.)

Others will take another path in which they too place their primary allegiance with Britain, but define themselves as *black* British. Those working towards this resolution will relate to elements in common between themselves and native whites including language and litera-ture, shared moral values and a common Western philosophy. Britain is home. They are likely to be aware of the evils of their particular historic roles in British affairs, but place an emphasis on their achievements against the odds. They will be realistic about colour prejudice, reacting overtly to its appearance and otherwise relating to people on their merits.

West Indian girls in Bristol differ from the boys in important ways. The study shows that they are likely to have conflicted identifications with their parents as well as with general representatives of their own ethnicity; their ethnicity features doubly, within and beyond the family. But, unlike the boys, they do not manifest generally high levels of identification conflicts with native whites. Hence, of all the adoles-cents considered so far, they will be the ones most involved with grappling with the meaning of their own ethnicity. They are therefore individuals who may most radically redefine their roles within their ethnic group. Yet theirs is likely to be a difficult task, because of their doubly conflictual identifications with those closest to them.

Some of these young women of Caribbean parentage are likely to be in the vanguard of informal social movements which modify the life-styles that would have been passed on from their parental genera-tion. They are likely to develop imaginative and formidable syntheses of identity elements. Yet some of them are likely to become short-term casualties – adolescent girls who find themselves adrift in levels of identification conflicts too great to tolerate. Other evidence from this same study (Weinreich, 1975b) demonstrates that some West Indian girls manifest high levels of identification conflicts dispersed across many significant others (that is, high *identity diffusion* to use Erikson's term). Since, however, they also appear to be more able to ac-knowledge higher levels of such conflict than West Indian boys, they are likely to pass through acute phases of difficulty more rapidly than the boys.

Additional empirical evidence shows that these girls identify more closely with their peers as positive role models than with adults (this does not hold for West Indian boys, nor for English and Asian boys and girls in the Bristol sample). The rapid formation of new peer-group consensuses would be a potent factor giving support to new self-conceptions. Their assertiveness and rejection of traditional roles will probably pose a threat to some young West Indian men. Whilst many of these West Indian adolescent males concern themselves with roots and allegiances, many of their female counterparts are likely to proceed towards potent conceptions of themselves as black British.

In these analyses of potential self-concept change using the Bristol data, predictions are derived from a knowledge of the differing distributions between ethnic and, in the case of the West Indian adolescents, sex groups. The theoretical principle which has been applied throughout is that people will strive to resolve their identification conflicts. In nearly all cases of these minority group adolescents their own ethnicity plays a salient role in their identity development in that it is a shared feature of their identification conflicts, whatever the other differences. The analyses, crude though they are being at the aggregate group level, point to a considerable diversity of potential self-concept changes especially among West Indian adolescents. Despite the limitations of sample size and restriction to one geographical location, the study suggests some of the likely developments which may be expected to occur, ones that will bring about social changes in relationships between individuals of different ethnicities and between generations within ethnic groups.

By being explicit about the loci of identification conflicts with others, the analyses provide a more specific understanding of what underlies 'identity conflict' and 'culture conflict' (see C. Ballard, this volume). It is seen that conflicts in ethnic identification in minority group adolescents are unexceptional, but that they are not synonymous with 'problems'. The evidence shows no *general* demoralisation of these adolescents compared with native whites. Whilst psychological disturbances may be manifest within particular individuals (who would require appropriate care), it would be misleading to generalise from such cases to the group as a whole.

It is evident that interactions between people of different ethnic groups will be complex and changing. Attempted negotiations in self-concept development, that is, the presentation of self in novel or unusual ways, may be open to misinterpretation by others and perceived as affronts to conventional norms. If, as a result, the legitimate concerns of adolescents from ethnic minorities are thwarted by 'responsible' representatives of the indigenous population, such as teachers, employers, the police or politicians, behavioural conflicts will be inevitable. The legitimacy derives from the fact that such adolescents are not aliens, but people who are responsive to important values articulated (even if not always practised) by influential indigenous people, values such as fair play, opportunity to realise one's potential, standing up for one's rights, or whatever they may be in individual cases. Their responsiveness is indicated by the almost universal salience of their ethnic identification conflicts, which it is argued will cause them to strive towards redefinitions of their own ethnicity. Notwithstanding their own ethnic distinctiveness, they are segments of changing British sub-cultures in which most changes are the outcomes of the changing self-concepts of native whites. Whilst the ethnic component does not feature in the same way for the native white adolescents as it does for the West Indian and the Asian adolescents, they too have identification conflicts, the attempted resolutions of which will involve changes in their self-concepts. The overall context for social change and changing self-definitions remains primarily with the changing inter-relationships within the total social structure, of which ethnic minorities form a small part only.

Policy implications

The study provides a perspective on questions of 'identity conflict' and 'culture conflict' which indicates that more refined concepts than these are required for an understanding of the processes of self-concept development in a multi-ethnic context. It is seen that ethnicity plays a central part in the self-concept of the Asian and West Indian adolescents sampled, but in a way that is interactive with the values of the broader community.

The traditional view of Asian separateness in encapsulated communities is brought into question by the changes which are taking place in the Asian adolescents' images of themselves. Concrete evidence of widespread changes in attitudes between Asian adolescents and their parents in Britain is contained in a study by the Community Relations Commission (1976), which documents the discrepancies between *current* attitudes held by both sections of various Asian communities in different regions. However, the changes should not be seen as ones of wholehearted assimilation to, or endorsement of English life-styles, but as redefinitions of their ethnic distinctiveness. This will set them apart from their more entrenched elders, but not from the Asian communities in general.

West Indian adolescents in Bristol are unlikely to develop the cohesiveness of the Asians. Instead, it is argued that the boys are likely to diverge in their self-conceptions, and that some of the girls are likely to be prominent social changers. Hence, it would be a mistake to perceive them in uniform terms. Aggregate statistics concerning West Indian adolescents (on delinquency, educational achievement, etc.) would need to be interpreted with care to prevent generalisations that ignored the diversity of emerging self-conceptions. In their attempts to resolve their identification conflicts some boys may adopt 'back to Africa' symbolism (including Rastafarian locks), some Pentecostalism, and some an assertive Black British stance. Some of the girls are likely to pose a strong challenge to their traditionalist elders. One challenge to orthodoxy may be to assert 'adult' femininity through child-bearing, another to assert self-sufficiency and independence through their earning power.

It is recommended that the terms 'culture conflict' and 'identity conflict' be sparingly used. They are imprecise terms. When applied to the consequences of contact between different cultures, they falsely stigmatise whole groups of people as 'social problems'. Whilst some adolescents of immigrant parentage may go through acute phases of psychological distress, there are positive pay-offs in the contributions of creative resolutions of identification conflicts to social change. Social change may, of course, result in behavioural conflict, as when, for example, minority group adolescents increasingly assert their opposition to prejudice and discrimination. In this case, conflict arises from the discrepancy between societally proclaimed values of citizenship and the lack of their day-to-day implementation. That is, the 'social problem' is within the indigenous community, not the minority, and disappears when the same citizenship rights are respected for all, including minorities, on an everyday basis.

The position expressed here concerning the location of 'social problems' is at variance with that presented recently by the Community Relations Commission: 'It is clear that young Asians need help to overcome the growing tensions between them and their parents and the wider community. We make the following recommendations to the Asian community and to the public agencies for tackling the causes of the problems' (Community Relations Commission, 1976, p. 60). The problems are implicitly defined by the Community Relations Commission as being within the Asian community and requiring special help from outside.

Yet a principal source of conflict between Asian youth and others would be removed given the absence of prejudice and victimisation, a problem not of their making. If tensions between generations are perceived as causes of problems their magnitude should be kept in perspective. Such tensions tend to exist in all communities, since they are in part the result of changing values accompanying the normal processes of adolescent self-concept development. There is no evidence that they are greater in minority communities, only that they are based in different issues, ethnicity being a salient one as this study and the Community Relations Commission study show.

If professional agencies are inadequately prepared for recognising newly arising circumstances, they are faced with 'problems' of their own. Perhaps too often these are perceived as coming from within minority groups rather than from deficiencies in societal institutions. As an example, the teacher in the class room needs the back-up resources of a counselling service which could provide an understanding of self-concept developments in adolescents from different communities. If adolescent 'affronts' to authority are seen instead as expressions of self-presentation with particular historic and cultural roots, teacher and student may achieve a more effective understanding (see Driver, this volume). Few teachers with heavy teaching commitments could probe such relationships alone. Counselling services in schools could alleviate feelings of impotence amongst teachers and inadequacy amongst students by providing the resources for coping with individual distress and a forum for generating an awareness of self-concept development in a multi-ethnic context. The expected pay-off would be more productive teaching and fewer referrals to child guidance clinics or special schools.

5

Having tackled the popular notion of 'identity conflict' we move to the population of South Asians in Britain to challenge another popular misconception and to consider how it hinders understanding and impedes the provision of useful support by individuals and institutions. 'Helpers' in touch with Asian adolescents perceive their problem in terms of a clash between two cultures, a 'culture conflict'. Their misunderstanding of the dynamics of the real situation, and the provision of inappropriate supportive measures for those in need of help may cause new stresses rather than alleviate existing ones. The adolescents' difficulties are aggravated when popular currency is given to the problematic connotations of difference, and to the simplistic assumption that minority adolescents should belong to one 'culture' or the other, because no healthy synthesis of the two is feasible.

This paper describes the likely sources of conflict within the South Asian family and explains how many adolescents maintain and adapt traditional values and allegiances despite external pressures to the contrary. The strength of the socialisation process and community pressures are reinforced by the adolescents' response to the rejection and prejudice of 'outsiders'. The stresses experienced by minorities are not only the product of migration or the meeting of two cultures; they may be brought on the minority by the misconceptions of the dominant majority.

Conflict, Continuity and Change

Second-generation South Asians

Catherine Ballard

Much discussion of the second generation of South Asians[1] in Britain takes as its starting point an assumption that there are major and increasingly irresolvable conflicts between them and their parents. The emphasis is placed on the incompatibility of Asian and Western culture and on the discontinuities and contradictions in the behaviour and aspirations of the two generations. It is widely believed that Asian children will grow up to desire all the freedom of their British peers and that they will challenge what is seen as the 'authoritarian repressiveness' of their parents. Young Asians are conceptualised by the British as a rootless generation who are caught between two cultures. The media sensationalise only the casualties among them: those who have run away from home, who have attempted suicide, who have been returned to India or Pakistan against their will or who have been beaten up, even murdered, by their fathers. As a result of these commonly held British attitudes, when British teachers, doctors or social workers try to help young Asians who are in difficulties they often assume that 'culture conflict' must be the root of the problem.

This definition sets young Asians apart as a 'problem' category, often failing to recognise that there can be a comparable degree of conflict between parents and children in families of any cultural background. It does not take into account the particular personalities of individuals within the families concerned nor their various material and social circumstances. More seriously, it assumes that cultural values are fixed and static and that there is no possibility of adaptation, flexibility or accommodation between one set of values and another. However, the outsider who attempts to help with an inter-generational crisis in an Asian family is faced with serious difficulties.

He is likely to find himself handicapped by a lack of understanding of the complexity of the cultural factors involved, by the difficulty of communicating with the parents and by the strange half-British half-Asian behaviour of the children. It is perhaps not suprising that the helping outsider is tempted to advise the adolescent to escape from the situation by leaving home.

This paper sets out to put such cases into perspective by showing how the majority of young Asians in Britain (those who are not, at present, getting into serious difficulties) are coming to terms with their situation. The material on which it is based has been drawn from five years of social anthropological field-work carried out among Sikh families in Leeds and in their villages of origin in Punjab.[2] During the course of field-work, close contact has been maintained with a number of young Asians, some of them Hindu and some Moslem, in the period of their transition from adolescence to adulthood. Only a very small proportion of them have faced critical problems of the kind described above. A much greater number did go through a period of upheaval within their families which temporarily caused them intense personal distress and strong feelings of alienation. However, these problems were usually resolved within the family without any evidence of long-lasting bitterness or disruption.[3]

It is argued in this paper that many of the second generation of Asians in Britain may rebel against their parents' social and cultural values during their teens. The resulting clashes may lead some of them to seek outside help and support at this time. Yet by their late teens and early twenties the majority of them do largely conform to Asian behavioural norms within the sphere of family and community life. Their 'Asian-ness' is inevitably different in some respects from that of their parents. They have been brought up in, and have greater access to, British society. Many have reacted not only to unacceptable features of British culture, but also to negative attitudes and discriminatory behaviour on the part of the British. This paper attempts to show how and why only a small number of second generation Asians actually reject, or wish to reject, their families and communities completely. It uses illustrations from the experiences of informants and quotes their own words wherever possible. First, the socialisation of Asian children is briefly described. The paper then illustrates the kinds of inter-generational conflicts which may occur and how these may be resolved. Finally the extent to which such conflicts can be attributed to cultural features is examined and the usefulness of the popular concept of 'culture conflict' is assessed.

In attempting to describe regularities and to detect overall patterns in the behaviour of second generation Asians some generalisation has been necessary. The more extreme and unrepresentative experiences have been ignored, and there is no consideration here of the differences between migrants from different areas. While there are obvious variations between Indian, Pakistani and Bangladeshi communities in Britain, between those that have come via East Africa and also between Asian settlements in different British cities, the overall similarities are striking in comparison with British culture. It is this general category 'Asian' which is used throughout this paper.

Children at home

Most second-generation Asians in Britain are being brought up by parents whose own upbringing was in rural India, Pakistan and Bangladesh. In the sub-continent households are often large and several adults share the responsibility for making decisions affecting the family, for running the household and family economy and for caring for the children. Within the village each household is part of a tightly knit community of close kinsmen. Social change is slow in rural areas and, at least until recently, there has been no expectation of the need for significant differences in behaviour from one generation to the next. The experience of adults is directly relevant to their children. Boys are trained to run the family farm or to practise their hereditary craft and girls learn the domestic skills expected of a good wife and mother. They learn through gradually increasing participation in the work of the household, and by their early teens they play a significant part in the domestic economy. The toys which they play with in childhood are miniatures of the tools and utensils which adults use or natural materials available in the village and the surrounding fields. For most children education is the acquisition through very formal teaching of basic skills in reading, writing and arithmetic. Relationships within the family are affectionate but hierarchical: great emphasis is placed on respect for elders, on restraint in relations between the sexes and on maintaining the honour and good name of the family. The interests of the group as a whole always take precedence over those of the individual members. Within the group roles are clearly defined, goals are shared and no great emphasis is placed on the development of an exclusive personal identity.

Asian households in Britain may often be smaller than those in the villages of the sub-continent, because very often only a section of the family has settled in Britain. As time passes however, and as sons grow up, marry and have children of their own, the household begins to increase in size. Many families make great efforts to remain together, but the small size of most British houses often makes it necessary to establish several residential and domestic units, although the ties between them may remain very close. It is still common for young couples to spend the first few years of their married life living with the boy's parents, and invariably one son and his wife and children will continue to live with them, even if others move out. It is extremely rare to find elderly people living on their own. Households where two brothers and their families live together are also by no means unusual. Chain migration, where early settlers called relatives to join them, has ensured that almost every family has an extensive network of kinsmen living in Britain. Frequently many of them will live in the same area, but the exigencies of the employment and housing markets usually mean that they will be geographically scattered. None the less the concept of being part of a large kinship group, with its concomitant loyalties and obligations, remains very strong. Residential units may be small and kinship groups fragmented and scattered but there is constant visiting and contact between them. The kinship group with its common identification with the village or areas of origin is still the most important focus of social interaction (see Saifullah Khan, this volume).

An Asian child in Britain learns very early in its life that it is part of a wide and stable family group. The bonds of affection within this group, the security which it provides for its members and the group's sense of its own identity are very strong. From its earliest infancy a child will receive attention and care from a number of adults and older siblings. Even if the household is small, its members will spend much time exchanging visits with relatives and friends who, in the absence of the full kinship group, take on the role of quasi-kin. Small children are constantly carried, cuddled and kept amused and there is little separation of adult and child activities. The smallest children are taken on all family outings, they are present at all ceremonies and they are not sent away when adult functions and discussions are taking place. Allowances are made for children, but their needs are not seen as being very different from the rest of the family. They are participants in all family events and because of this they learn to behave responsibly at an early age. They learn by example and through play, which often imitates adult activity, the behaviour which will be expected of them as they grow up. Imitative play gradually develops into real help, so that by the time a child is seven or eight years old it will be taking an important part in the work of the household, looking after smaller children, performing minor domestic tasks and helping to entertain guests. As a member of the family group the child is expected to share everything with others. The emphasis is always on 'we' and 'ours' rather than on 'I' and 'mine' and the demanding of exclusive attention from parents is not greatly encouraged.

We have to start reminding them that they're not alone in the family from the time when they're very small. For instance, if my littlest one wants some sweets then I say that if he has them he'll have to share them with his brothers and sisters. That's how we do it, showing them that they have to think of others before themselves. Otherwise there's no hope for our kind of family. (*Sikh father*)

An Asian child's experience of the mutual co-operation which binds the family together is very intense, and constant exposure to the social life of the community is very effective conditioning. By the time children enter school they have been socialised into a very different set of values from those of their British peers.

School and the outside world

Many Asian parents find British education very mystifying and they fear its effect on their children. Pre-school education, the lack of formality in school, the free mixing of the sexes, the idea that children learn at their own speed and not by rote are all unfamiliar notions. In the schools of the sub-continent children are generally not encouraged to be questioning and assertive or to develop their own aptitudes in their own way. Careers tend to be chosen because of the prestige or perquisites which they might bring to the family in the long term. When asked what he felt about his education here, a Sikh father said:

I'd really like to send my children to school in India, you know. It would be better for them, because the teacher would beat them to make sure that they learned their lessons. Here it's terrible the way children play around all day and don't learn quickly at all. I'll agree that higher education is better here, that's after the tenth class in India, about age 16, but it's not good until then.

English family life is also puzzling and threatening to many Asian parents. It seems insecure and cold and there appears to be little respect for the older generation. Marriages break up, old people go into homes and children into care for what seem to be the flimsiest of reasons, and sexual licence is visible everywhere. Such behaviour is inhumane and outrageous by Asian standards.

The second generation participate in the British educational system and they are exposed to the values of their British peers. A gulf between them and their parents is inevitable, but it is usually neither so wide nor so clear-cut as outsiders may assume. Intense socialisation in the family and the community means that most young Asians value the supportiveness, economic co-operation and clear morality which their families provide. They generally treat the elders of the family with respect and recognise that maintaining the family's good name is in the interests of all its members. They may disagree very strongly with their parents over specific issues and may envy the freedom and independence of British teenagers, but many young Asians feel strongly that too much freedom leads to confusion and unhappiness. They are critical of the casualness of British attitudes to family responsibility and educational success and believe that obligations should be taken seriously:

I have to behave differently at home than I do at college, like I can't dress in really fashionable clothes and of course I can't smoke. But I don't want to because I'm proud of my family and being Indian, and I don't want to give that up. I don't mind taking orders from my brother, in fact it's right that I should. He's paying for my education and he trusts me to do well for the sake of the family. (*Dentistry student*)

You shouldn't see the joint family as just an economic group, all of us living together so that we can share everything and live cheaply. It's much more a matter of the love and respect that we have for each other and the fact that we all decide things together. (*Sixth-former*)

Sometimes I'm really shocked by the way English families behave. I was in a pub one night and this lad came up to his father and said 'Hello, how are you getting along?' His Dad just said 'I'm O.K.' – they didn't seem much interested in each other. Then he said, 'Buy us a pint, son' and the lad said 'Not bloody likely, buy it yourself!' I was staggered, can you imagine that in a Punjabi family?' (*Apprentice*)

All that the girls at work talk about is boys and sex and their figures. Sometimes I'm quite jealous of them being able to do whatever they want and I do enjoy their jokes. But I think they've got too much freedom and they just go and fall pregnant and have to marry lads who won't really care for them. There's not much happiness in that. (*Girl machinist*)

Asian children carry with them a deep sense of family loyalty and an awareness of their own cultural distinctiveness. Nevertheless, the contradictions between the assumptions on which their family relationships are based and many of the values with which they become familiar at school and through television, magazines and newspapers inevitably sharpen as they get older. There are many parallels between the critical and rebellious attitudes of Asian and Western adolescents. They may argue with their parents about the same things but by their mid teens young Asians are under particular stress. The orientation of their parents' lives may be increasingly exposed as being remote from the British norms with which they are becoming familiar. They may criticise their parents' rejection of British cultural styles. They become less willing to accept the unquestioned beliefs and assumptions of their parents, particularly as their education encourages them to demand explicit rationales for everything. For example, they begin to question the relevance and meaning of elaborate social and religious rituals, the segregation of the sexes and dietary restrictions. These may seem particularly strange because they belong to a way of life which the children themselves may never have experienced in the totality of its original context. Well-educated, intellectually enquiring children may be able to obtain only an unsatisfyingly fragmented understanding of their own culture. They may discover that many of their parents' beliefs and values do not stem directly from the tenets of their religion, but are a matter of local convention and have little meaning outside the village setting. The only image which they have of the totality of Asian culture, unless of course they spent the first part of their childhood in the sub-continent, is that presented by the glossy, romantic Indian and Pakistani musical films. Their presentation of both rural and urban life is extremely idealised, but none the less they do transmit many of the basic values of Asian society in a direct and graphic way. Some of them are dramatisations of religious and mythological stories and they are also an important medium for the transmission of language.

As children grow older they are expected to take a more prominent part in the social and religious life of their families and communities. At the same time, parents may put great pressure on them to work hard at school, as they often have very high expectations of their children. There are almost invariably arguments about the children's requests to go out with friends after school, to take part in extra-curricular activities and to wear fashionable clothes. Children may object strongly to having to spend so much time visiting relatives, participating in ceremonies and attending the Gurdwara, Mandir or Mosque regularly. However for the most part such arguments continue to take place within the framework of at least some shared values. Most young Asians try to avoid open conflict with their parents, not so much because they are physically fearful of them, but rather because they feel that they ought to obey their parents and to avoid dishonouring the family (see Weinreich, this volume).

Parents and children

If children too openly challenge their authority, parents may find it hard to respond with tolerance. They may find it extremely difficult to explain why they are unwilling to allow their children the intellectual and physical freedom which they demand. For them the village is still the point of reference and village structures have been replicated by the close-knit and inward-looking Asian communities in British cities. Even if parents are sympathetic to the aspirations of their children, they are very much aware that unconventional behaviour would almost certainly precipitate a great deal of critical comment. Gossip is an important sanction against non-conformity and its effect is feared almost as much by the second generation as by their parents.

Girls are under stricter surveillance than boys, for it is felt that too much freedom might spoil a girl's reputation and thus damage her chances of making a good marriage. In addition the status and prestige of the family as a whole depends upon keeping its reputation, much of which rests with the chaste behaviour of its women, irreproachable. Many girls complain about the dual standard of morality which allows their brothers a good deal more freedom than they have themselves:

> In Asian society the woman is a white piece of cloth, the man a black piece. If there are any dirty marks on the black cloth it will be difficult to see, but this won't be the case with the white cloth. The dirty marks will be seeen. (*Girl typist*)

However, if he goes too far, a boy's behaviour may also make it difficult for a good match to be made for himself or for his sisters. Every story about an Asian girl running away from home, and such stories are often featured in the Asian newspapers which are published in Britain, increases the anxiety of all parents about the corrupting influence of British norms on their own daughters. They may withdraw their daughters from school and speed up the arrangement of their marriages.

Such attempts to maintain control may, in fact, be counterproductive, for they may increase the girl's wish to break away. A clever girl was taken away from school before 'O' level and sent to work in a clothing factory under the watchful eye of women from her own community. She found the work so boring that she spent her time dreaming about eloping with a boy. Some parents are now beginning to see that allowing their daughters to stay on at school, obtain good qualifications and get married later may, in the end, be a better solution. As yet however, not all parents accept the value of educating their daughters beyond school-leaving age and many of them still react to signs that their children might be growing out of their control with strict measures. Although affection and understanding between parents and children may break down completely, sometimes with dramatic and disastrous results, it must be stressed that polarisation of the generations is by no means inevitable. At the moment many, indeed probably most, Asian families succeed in maintaining fairly good relations between the generations.

Some parents who understand the need for change and can communicate the reasons for their attitudes to their children are able to strike a balance between strict discipline and giving in to all their children's demands.

> We have to work very hard to educate them, to show them what's right in our view. If we let our children forget all about their Indian background and be just like the English, they'll get lost, they won't be really one or the other. We don't get anywhere by being too strict. If we try to control them too closely they'll just leave home, they won't respect us anymore. (*Sikh father*)

Some families share a deep religious faith, and parents and children are able to accept their differences calmly and to maintain mutual respect and affection.

> My father was a very religious man, a really good man, always helping other people. He always trusted me and didn't ask too many questions, even at the time when I was up to all sorts of things that he wouldn't have liked. Now I try to follow his example because although my life isn't like his, I mean I'm quite English in a lot of ways, I do respect him and his way too. (*Technician*)

Other parents are afraid of recognising the truth and they may turn a blind eye to what their children are doing, often confronting them over minor issues and avoiding the major ones. A father allowed his daughter to train as a nurse and never objected to the fact that night duty on the casualty ward was a part of her job. Yet when an insurance salesman called at their house this man was furious to find that his daughter invited the salesman into the house and was talking to him unchaperoned. The girl was very amused by the fact that her father had obviously not allowed himself to think seriously about the kind of encounters which she had with men as part of her work. In this case, as in many others, parents are prepared to allow their children considerable freedom when this is necessary for their careers but they may still demand that they should behave in a very orthodox way at home.

The fact that many Asian parents find themselves culturally and linguistically handicapped when they come into contact with British people and British institutions can have far-reaching effects on the balance of authority in the family. Parents may come to rely heavily on their children as interpreters and as sources of information. They may feel that they lack the knowledge to give guidance to their children about their education or employment. This situation can lead to some degree of breakdown in the hierarchical relationships which characterise the Asian family in the rural sub-continent. It may enable the second generation to challenge some of their parents' assumptions and, while keeping up an outward show of respect, to negotiate more freedom for themselves.

There is almost invariably inter-generational suspicion and argument in families with adolescent children. Severe and prolonged tension, where there seems to be little possibility of compromise, generally occurs when there are pre-existing factors within the family which makes it particularly vulnerable. Many family crises stem from the excessive authoritarianism of the father, whose behaviour may be partly the result of living in Britain. A man who finds himself in sole control of his family in a morally and socially alien setting with no model of authority to follow, may attempt to block all his children's attempts to be autonomous and independent and may even resort to verbal and physical violence. The discipline which he tries to exert may be inconsistent and his own confusion gives his children nothing concrete to assert themselves against or to conform to. An extreme example of this was that of a Gujerati father of four sons and two daughters, aged between seventeen and twenty-six. About two years after arriving in Britain this man became increasingly critical of his children's behaviour and of what he saw to be the British way of life. He became more and more isolated from his friends and kinsmen, although he had previously been a sociable man. As one of his sons put it, 'now all they get from him is long lectures condemning everyone and everything'. Much of the material for these diatribes came from his monitoring of 'sex and violence' programmes on television from which he constructed his own picture of the Western world. As well as verbally abusing his family he resorted to sporadic outbreaks of great violence. The police were called to the house several times. During the course of his first five years in Britain three of his sons left home at least once. The result of this man's behaviour was to achieve precisely what he set out to avoid, that is his children's alienation from him and their loss of interest in the values which he was trying to impart. Such cases are rare and most Asian parents are aware of the danger of behaviour of this kind, yet a few Asian fathers can be seen to be adopting extreme methods of enforcing their authority.

The mother's traditional role is to provide an example for her children to follow and to act as mediator between them and their father. In some families the mother finds it very difficult to pass on behavioural norms to her children when she is away from the context of the village and overwhelmed by domestic responsibility. She may find herself unable to understand, let alone answer, her children's questions or act as go-between for them and their father. She may become an increasingly remote, incomprehensible and negative figure to her children, withdrawing into religious ritual and prayer or becoming severely depressed. A few families are characterised by an almost total breakdown of ordinary relationships. This is frequently associated with poverty, overcrowding or mental and physical ill health affecting the family. The reaction of outside agencies to families of this sort may be that the problems are 'Asian' and that they cannot deal with them. However, once the cultural gloss has been removed, the real problems may be seen to be fundamentally no different from those of many British families in the case loads of social workers.

Approaches to outsiders

If conflict with parents becomes too serious to be endured, Asian teenagers may go to a British teacher, doctor or friend to explain their confusion and frustration. A sympathetic listener may be able to help to clarify the issues involved, to suggest strategies for dealing with the situation or to mediate between parents and children. However, in some cases the preconceptions of the outsider about Asian culture may cause them to take a completely one-sided view of the situation. Individuals who begin by seeking advice and help from 'outsiders' may increase their difficulties by accepting an external definition of what is happening. For example, in one extreme case a Pakistani girl greatly over-dramatised her problems with her parents in order to maintain the involvement of a number of concerned outsiders. None of them was able to give her any really effective help because they could not understand what her parents' position might be, and it became increasingly difficult for them to deduce how real her problems actually were. Finally it became clear that their involvement was worsening the situation by making it possible for the girl to sustain and exaggerate her problems, and particularly the Asian aspects of those problems, while continually passing the responsibility for solving them to outsiders.

Given complex cultural differences it is easy for outsiders to forget that a phase of rebellion against parental values and authority is an almost universal phenomenon, a part of the process of self-discovery in the transition from childhood to adulthood. A period of conflict does not necessarily signify a wish to break with the family for good. A proportion of teenagers from any background are temporarily driven to despair and need outside help with their problems. Critics of Asian culture, and particularly of the arranged marriage, often express strong objections to the way in which they feel that restrictions are placed on the freedom of young Asians by their families. Yet the same view is not taken when British teenagers come, in large part, to fulfil their parents' expectations after a period of rebellion. If it is assumed that differences in cultural values and expectations between Asian parents and children are irreconcilable, it seems to follow that the only solution for a young Asian who is in conflict with his parents is to move away from home. If advice to move out is taken it may often create greater difficulties in the long run:

> Things got so bad at home after they found out about my boyfriend that I thought I was going to have a breakdown and I went to the doctor for some pills. He's a nice man and really kind to me. He told me that leaving home was the best thing that I could do and he lent me £5 so that I could move to a hostel straight away. I had three sleepless nights there and then I went back home. I couldn't stand being alone. I missed my family terribly in spite of all the rows. I knew that by sleeping away from home I might be getting myself into real trouble for the future. Who's going to want to marry a girl who has run away? When I tried to explain to my doctor why I'd gone back he thought that I was barmy or that my parents had threatened me. He's never been quite the same to me since. He just didn't get it. (*Girl clerk*)

This girl, like many others, went through a period when the pressures of two contradictory sets of values on her became very stressful. She longed for more freedom, but when it was offered to her she found it empty and meaningless. She wanted the independence to make decisions for herself, but recognised that this might lead to loss of support from her family and community. Asian families provide security and warmth, yet pressure to conform can seem suffocating. Involvement in the affairs of their own families binds young Asians into constricting and time-consuming networks of mutual obligation, but they too can derive support from these networks. They know that they are very unlikely to find comparable support and affection if they break with their families. Asian children in British schools acquire some familiarity with British culture – they might well know more about St George and the dragon than about Guru Gobind Singh. Knowlege of their own culture, however fragmented, remains the framework of their family and social experience. Each individual responds to these contradictions in a different way and there is a great range of behaviour along the continuum from traditional to Western norms.

Most young Asians are able to participate effectively in both cultural systems. This may mislead outsiders into believing that the 'British' self which is presented to them is the whole picture. An example of this is the case of an articulate and sophisticated Hindu girl who opted to do a course in Physical Education at College. On realising that her parents, with whom she was living, might disapprove strongly of this, she went to tell her tutor that she had changed her mind. His response was to tell her that she could leave home and find digs near the college. It was very difficult for her to explain to him that she accepted her situation and had no wish to change it. Some informants were able to describe the way in which they play different roles in different situations:

> I've learned to behave as two different people. I'm quite another person when I'm away from home with English people than when I'm here with my family and my Punjabi friends. I'm so used to switching over that I don't even notice. I don't have any trouble getting along with English people, but I suppose though that I'm really Punjabi at heart. Sometimes I get very depressed when I'm at college. I long to get home and be Indian (*Pharmacology student*)

> I'm now pretty good at getting on with English people in their kind of way, but I love going home to Indian family life. I'd like to be more independent though, my parents won't even let me go hitch-hiking. And I'd like to go out with Indian girls in the English way.

But I know I'm mixed up over that. I'd be furious if I found that my sister was going out with a boy. (*Trainee engineer*)

Although they may have the skill to operate within two cultural worlds, most young Asians feel, like the boys quoted above, that their deepest loyalties are to their own group. They may experiment with a wide range of patterns of behaviour, but it is significant that by the time they reach secondary school most Asian children appear to have their closest friendships with other Asians. Interaction with British people and conformity with the dominant social style is unavoidable at school, college or work. However, most young Asians spend the greater part of their leisure time in the company of Asian peers, where rather different cultural styles are employed.

Decisions about marriage

All young Asians are very well aware throughout their childhood and adolescence that it is their parents' intention to arrange a marriage for them. As they approach the time when they complete their education and begin to earn a living, discussion of prospective matches becomes realistic and serious. When this occurs, they begin to realise the enormous significance of the impending match. Not only is it a matter of them being given a partner for life, but it is also an event which forces each individual to come to a decision and make a clear public statement about where his or her loyalties ultimately lie. This has important implications for their whole future life-style. Many of the arguments between children and their parents are not so much about the choice of spouse or the style of the wedding, but about the wider consequences of conformity.

During the period before their marriages are arranged some young people go out with boy or girl friends without parental permission. Some maintain that they will only marry for love, but very few have actually done this:

I used to manage to get out of the house almost every night to meet the Pakistani boy from next door but one. If my mother had ever known she would have had a fit and sent me straight back to the village. I was mad keen to be with him. We planned to run away together when I was older. I was full of romantic dreams and thought that I was quite fit to decide my future for myself. It's just as well that he went off me. (*Indian girl describing her behaviour at fifteen. She has recently had an arranged marriage.*)

Some are able to defer the arrangement of their marriage for some time, because they do not yet feel ready to commit themselves:

A couple of times my parents arranged for these boys and their families to come to our house to see me. Well, I used to make myself look a bit unattractive and stupid, you know, so that they wouldn't want me. (*Girl packer*)

Others, perhaps the majority, have always been clear about the ultimate limitations on their freedom of choice:

I've had loads of girlfriends, some English, some Indian, but I've always known that in the end I'd do what the family expected and marry the girl that they choose. I'm quite happy about that, in fact it's quite a relief. (*Mechanic*)

As the intensity of the pressure from the family increases, it becomes difficult to hold out against it:

I suppose I didn't want to get married at all, I couldn't imagine it happening to me. I liked my life as it was, where I was free to do what I wanted. But my Mum never talked about anything but girls, and how happy she'd be if I was married, and how everyone was gossiping about me being twenty-four and not even engaged. We went to see quite a few girls, but I turned them all down whatever they looked like. Then in the end it all got too much, so I said yes. I remember thinking at the time that at least she'd be useful as a chapatti maker. It hasn't turned out like that at all though. I get on really well with my wife and we go out together a lot. (*Technician*)

Outside observers often do not perceive that an arranged marriage must be seen within the context of prior socialisation and established kinship networks. Acceptance of such a marriage can be seen as symbolising an individual's loyalty and commitment to his family and community, and to all the personal advantages and disadvantages that this implies. Having gone through with the marriage and made this commitment, often with considerable foreboding, most young Asians come to feel that their parents' careful choice of a spouse has not been such a bad one and that they have more freedom than they expected. They usually also find themselves 'falling in love' with their husband or wife in the traditional Asian way, that is after the marriage ceremony rather than in a prior period of courtship. Some arranged marriages do end in disaster for a variety of reasons, but most Asians, including many of the second generation, would maintain that they are based on sounder foundations than 'love marriages' and that they are probably less likely to fail.

There is, however, now a great deal of pressure for the system to become more flexible. In Britain, as well as in the sub-continent, young Asians are now asking for, and often getting, the chance to meet one another properly, or at least to talk at length over the telephone, before the engagement takes place. Most of them are now able to veto a proposed match, but many would like to be able to choose from a number of prospective spouses. Many find the rules about the caste and clan into which one may or may not marry unreasonable, and the majority object strongly to marriage with a boy or girl who has just been brought over from the sub-continent. Yet few of the second generation show much interest in marriage with non-Asians, and many of the clandestine pre-marital relationships referred to above are, in fact, with other Asians. Sometimes an already established relationship can be presented as if it were a conventionally arranged marriage, so saving face for the family. Almost all marriages known to us among young Sikhs in Leeds, including those who lived away from home while they were at college, have been arranged by parents, although there have been some 'behind the scenes' negotiations of the kind just described. As long as families remain tightly organised, so that marriage is as much a contract between two families as between two individuals, it seems likely that family involvement in marriage will continue.

There have also been changes at the level of the closest interpersonal relationships among Sikhs in Leeds. Young married couples are building more egalitarian and romantic relationships with one another. They may go out together much more and place a higher value on their separate identities than did their parents. They may postpone the birth of their first child in order to give themselves time and freedom to get to know one another. However, initially even minor changes such as this may cause difficulties:

After we were married we decided that I would take the Pill for two or three years so that I could go on working and we could save some money, but mostly because we wanted to get about a bit and get used to being together. Of course I couldn't tell his mother, she was waiting to hear that I was expecting right from the start. Now it's coming up to two years since we were married, we're happy as we are, but I'm beginning to get some funny looks from the women around here and his mother keeps asking if I'm all right and everything. Now I've started getting scared, wondering if I ever will be able to start a baby and if I did wrong by going my own way and taking the Pill. And no one's going to sympathise with me. (*Girl packer*)

Most of the older generation still live within a world which is dominated by kinship relations, but the younger people are making friendships on the basis of compatibility. As they move towards a greater individualism, so they inevitably weaken the networks of kinship in terms of which their parents operate. Since the roots of the second generation are not in the rural sub-continent it seems likely that loyalty to fellow villagers, observation of the rules of caste, the seclusion of women and dietary prohibitions will begin increasingly to be disregarded. However, a medical student who came to Britain as a small child was not exceptional when he said: 'I'd never dream of missing a marriage of someone from our village. I'd always make sure that I got there, whatever I was doing. It's most important to me to be there.'

Racism and the growth of reactive ethnicity

The choice between Asian and British life-styles has so far been described in terms of negotiating a way through the contradictory pressures. There is, however, another pressure which is of critical importance in determining the choices which the second generation are making. Young Asians who have been brought up and educated in Britain are constantly aware of being 'different', and the experience of racial discrimination has the most profound effect on every individual. Even if they have lived here all their lives and are thoroughly familiar with, and competent in, British social styles, young Asians know that they will still be labelled 'immigrants' and 'Pakkis', that they will be treated as inferiors and that it will be very hard for them to obtain the most desirable employment and housing because of the significance put on the colour of their skins. Some are able to retell their experiences of discrimination and abuse with ironic humour, others recognise the general existence of racialism in Britain but find it intensely painful to admit that it has directly affected them. All sense that the issue of their colour is a component in all their relationships with British people. This adds a crucial new dimension to Asian ethnicity. While synthesising aspects of both Asian and British cultures some young Asians seem to be reacting to the rejection they experience from British society by taking renewed pride in their separate cultural identity. They may demonstrate this symbolically by re-adopting the wearing of the turban or the sari. Some are taking an increasingly serious interest in their own backgrounds and are arranging to visit their country of origin. A few are now taking the possibility of returning permanently seriously. They seek more scholarly information about their religion and customs than their parents are able to provide and some are learning their own language in its literary rather than its vernacular form. The result of personal, social and economic insecurity is to encapsulate Asians in their own communities. One effect of racial discrimination seems to be in checking the drift towards total Westernisation. This drift is frequently predicted as inevitable for the children and grandchildren of Asian migrants to Britain.

Many young Asians are feeling increasingly strongly that they should use their education and their knowledge of British society and politics in order to help their own groups. They are deeply dissatisfied with the way in which many of the 'leaders' of their communities, drawn largely from the first generation and often from the professional middle class, have failed to represent the feelings and experiences of the majority to outsiders. They believe that much stronger action should be taken to counter the discrimination and humiliation which they suffer. They regard many of the established Asian political organisations as ineffectual and unrelated to the needs of the second generation. They feel that as these organisations stand at present they have little to offer to the second generation. Increasing political awareness has not as yet, however, led to the formation of any very cohesive political groups.

Young Asians in Britain are obviously changing and adapting the traditions of their parents, but deeply-held feelings of loyalty to the family and community can change only slowly and may be reinforced in response to rejection from outside. They can move confidently in both the Asian and British worlds, but the majority continue to feel that their roots lie in the resources of Asian culture. They are seeking to reform and modify their parents' values rather than to move away from them completely:

> I used to feel that I was trapped in a kind of bubble. I couldn't seem to get away from our relatives and all the gossip and nattering and politics was unbelievable. It would have been easy for me to break out, I was ready to be off and marry an English girl or something to get right away. But I've come to see that I had more to lose than to gain by acting like that. There's a lot I really like about our way of doing things and anyway I could see that whatever I did I'd always be an outsider. The things I don't like I either take no notice of any more, or else I'm slowly getting away from them in my own life without being a rebel about it. (*Laboratory technician*)

The notion that young Asians are likely to 'suffer from culture conflict' is a gross oversimplification of a wide range of complex personal experiences. It assumes a straightforward clash, a tug-of-war, between East and West, traditional and modern, rural and urban, repression and freedom, resulting in an unbridgeable gulf between the generations. In reality, young Asians are not faced with an either/or situation. They have difficult dilemmas to resolve and in resolving them they work towards their own synthesis of Asian and British values. Implicit in the idea of 'culture conflict' are the ethnocentric assumptions that young Asians would like to 'be like us' if their parents would only let them and that Asian culture is in some way inferior and problematic.

Growing up in an Asian family in Britain does not itself cause stress. Many of the problems which do occur are not the result of conflicts caused by migration and the experience of great social change, but of external pressures. Living in inner city areas, where housing, schools and recreational facilities are poor, may give rise to tension and anxiety which are compounded by racial hostility. Young Asians are adept, as are most adolescents, at making compromises enabling them to deal with two parallel worlds. Their particular difficulty is that they are pioneers. Relevant models of adult behaviour are only now beginning to emerge as some of the second generation reach adulthood. Each individual still has to choose a workable middle course between a culture whose totality he has never experienced and a culture which ultimately rejects him as an unwanted alien. Many second-generation Asians are emphatic about their intention to give their own children a wider knowledge and clearer understanding of Asian culture than they had when they were children themselves. A tentative prediction for the future can perhaps be made from the widespread belief, which the second generation are coming increasingly to share with their parents, that contact with the sub-continent and familiarity with Asian social and cultural norms must be maintained. They know that they cannot have complete confidence in the world beyond their community in which they feel they will always be treated as outsiders. Their 'Asian-ness' however, as defined by them, is their ultimate security.[4]

6

The focus shifts here to the position of teachers who, like all practitioners, are constrained by the structures and situations within which they work. It is not simply the prevailing notions about children of minority status which limit the effectiveness of teachers in the classroom. Neither the historical development of the organisation and principles of education, nor the training of the teachers described here have been appropriate to the demands of a multi-cultural classroom. Because the teachers do not have the managerial and communication skills necessary in this new situation, they too experience stress in the classroom. This in turn, it is argued here, influences their attitudes to, and academic assessment of, their pupils.

The paper picks up the differences between West Indian boys and West Indian girls mentioned in Weinreich's paper in this volume. It illustrates the various means of support used by pupils in response to the situation in which they find themselves. It reminds us also of the various cultures within the externally imposed category 'West Indian' and the likelihood of one of these being predominant in any one particular setting.

Classroom Stress and School Achievement

West Indian adolescents and their teachers

Geoffrey Driver

This paper reviews briefly the development of both theoretical and practical resources used by British educators to deal with ethnic minority pupils whose presence has increased substantially in some schools since the 1950s. Drawing on the writer's own research,[1] it focuses on the skills of teachers in inter-personal negotiations with their ethnic minority pupils. The social and academic outcomes of classroom relations are considered and indicate that the teachers' skills of perception and communication appeared inadequate for the range of social expression demanded of them in interaction with West Indian, predominantly Jamaican, pupils.

The background debate

The development of 'multiracial' classrooms is comparatively recent. West Indian and South Asian children only began to attend British schools in any substantial numbers twenty years ago. This development has, however, affected only a limited number of schools serving the older residential districts in each of the country's main industrial conurbations. Such inner-city schools, rarely among the more educationally prestigious, were suddenly called upon to provide for the educational needs of children who, in a number of ways, were quite different from their forerunners. Until 1955, most teachers taught children whose native language was English. Over a short period of time there were many pupils in their class whose mother tongue was

Urdu or Punjabi and who spoke English only with difficulty. Teachers who thought they could understand every dialect in the English language found that they could not readily understand the *patois* which West Indian children often used in conversation with one another. In primary and secondary schools attended by these children, class sizes grew unexpectedly and their ethnic composition changed rapidly. Sometimes within a matter of ten years, West Indian or South Asian children have formed the largest ethnic category within the pupil population.

As these changes took place, the teachers and administrators of the schools involved became increasingly concerned to make special provision for their ethnic minority pupils. The problem appeared dramatic to those involved, but it was a localised phenomenon. For a long period there were no major national policy directives. Resources and research which could have been provided nationally at an early stage did not appear urgent on the national scale of priorities. It was local education authorities with responsibilities for the schools with increasing numbers of ethnic minority pupils who were compelled to develop locally-based resources, often without the benefit of any serious research and largely on the advice of teachers already heavily engaged in dealing with West Indian and South Asian pupils.

The action taken in these circumstances ought not to be underestimated, but the teachers' responses to their new pupils were necessarily immediate and experimental. When working groups of teachers and local authority inspectors came together to generate suitable curricular materials, their schemes were usually directed at helping their 'immigrant' pupils to catch up to the levels of basic skills, particularly in the use of spoken and written English. At this stage, the nature of the educational problems presented by these children was to provide them with the skills and qualifications which would enable them to become assimilated into British society.[2] Emotional problems exhibited by these children in school were thought to be simply the transient outworking of migration experiences. The professional judgement of many educators was that they could expect the need for special provision to diminish once the 'immigrant' children were 'born here'. In retrospect, it is easy to condemn these on-the-spot judgements. The teachers who made them were breaking new ground and had little backing, research or theory to orient their thinking.

Towards the end of the 1960s several theories appeared which were related to this field of education. In most cases they derived from research funded by American anti-poverty and anti-discrimination legislation during the Kennedy–Johnson presidential eras. As a result there were attempts in Britain, as in the United States, to correlate low levels of educational attainment with indices of social, economic and cultural deprivation, and to propose crash educational programmes geared to counter the influences of deprivation. Most of the serious problems of poverty in the big American cities were in areas where Black Americans were concentrated, and the theories about their intelligence and linguistic abilities (and disabilities) were seen by many observers as a compound of ethnic and socio-economic variables. This appeared to some to be applicable to the case of West Indians in Britain. However, these theoretical views have recently come under attack on both sides of the Atlantic. Today many critics and theorists take the view that the concept of an integrated society, in which its individual members are to be expected to conform to certain established socio-cultural norms, is unjustifiable. They reject the melting-pot theory which underlies concepts of relative social, cultural and linguistic 'disadvantage' as little more than political power play. In any case, they argue, efforts to assimilate ethnic minorities to the host population's cultural forms have been shown to be unworkable. As an alternative they propose social policies based on a pluralist model of society. In theory, pluralism calls for the corporate acceptance of ethnic minorities into the social and political fabric, rather than acceptance of ethnic minority members as individuals. In practice, it requires the recognition of a diversity of cultural forms and structures produced in a number of ethnic settings. In educational terms, this might well mean the acceptance and evaluation of pupils according to a range of criteria acceptable to their minority community's agreed and established formulae rather than criteria established for the total society.

The debate between the assimilationist approach and the pluralist position, although evident in general policy discussions, has made little impact on schools in Britain. Only a small minority of teachers seem prepared to acknowledge the validity of pluralist arguments. This was the situation in the West Midlands secondary school of this study, where all but a handful of the staff assumed that the only course, in either social or educational terms, was to assimilate the new ethnic minorities to the culture of the majority. No more than one or two of the ethnic minority pupils took this view. Indeed it can be argued that, despite the assumptions of the teachers concerning their task of facilitating assimilation, their relations with the various categories of West Indian (and South Asian) pupils served to heighten rather than decrease the sense of ethnic difference and consciousness. This situation is repeated in other secondary schools serving substantially West Indian and South Asian areas up and down the country.

The school and classroom

The writer's own research (Driver, 1977)[3] was concerned to document the institutional processes and outcomes, and personal experiences of members of one ethnic minority in school. The material discussed below is drawn from an ethnographic case study focusing upon a number of West Indian, predominantly Jamaican, boys and girls, aged about thirteen in 1971 and rising to about fifteen in 1973. They were all pupils in the same age-cohort, or form, in the same secondary modern school serving a West Midlands neighbourhood with a large West Indian minority population. The form contained about 140 pupils in all: 45 per cent of these were West Indians, 35 per cent were English and 20 per cent were South Asians. The majority of the West Indian pupils were from Jamaican families (around 60 per cent) and there were smaller numbers whose parents originated from St Kitts and Barbados, and a few from Trinidad. At most, three out of thirty-five teachers in this secondary modern school were other than English: one was a Bengali, one was a Barbadian and the other an American.

It was an important aspect of the study to compare the academic records of these pupils with their school and classroom experiences. To this end, assessment data accumulated on each pupil over the entire period of their post-primary education was documented and, during the three years of the study, the assessment procedures were carefully studied. The ethnographic account of the round of school and classroom life provided an important backdrop to the host of detailed events which took place in classrooms, corridors, the playground and elsewhere. The paper presents some important characteristics of social relations between English teaching staff and West Indian pupils, and suggests how these contributed to the formal outcomes of schooling for individual pupils (that is, their school achievement record up to and including the final school-leaving public examination results).

There are several aspects essential to the understanding of any classroom situation. These include the individual participants' (teacher and pupils) perceptions of their roles, their respective perceptions of their social situation and the main relationships outside the classroom to which individual participants are attached. In a 'multiracial' classroom, the situation is complicated by the fact that role perceptions, definitions of social situations, relationships outside the classroom and skills to express these perceptions may differ markedly between individual participants. Under such conditions, the chances for misunderstanding are very much higher than might normally be the case.

In the following paragraphs the special requirements, strains and responses involved in the teaching role of the 'multiracial' classrooms are considered. The outcomes of social relations between teachers and their West Indian pupils are then assessed.

The complexities of classroom management

The primary function of any teacher is to impart knowledge and skills in which he/she has received recognised qualifications, to pupils for whom such learning is deemed appropriate. The classroom role of a teacher goes beyond this. To maximise the learning that takes place, a teacher must establish conducive learning conditions. Thus the teacher is in part a social manager, as well as an instructor. School-teaching success depends substantially on the attainment of management skills if classroom social relations are to be an asset rather than a limitation in attaining the learning objectives of a particular curriculum.

The most common example of the difficulties experienced in executing the double role of a classroom teacher is that of any student teacher out on first teaching practice. His/her lesson plans and teaching methods may be well considered and identical with those of a more experienced colleague, but he/she will almost certainly be inexperienced in managing classroom relations. The mastery of those relations consists in subtleties of observation, information and action: knowing individuals by name and personality, discerning pupils' moods and intentions in the briefest glimpses of expressions and gestures, weighing up the potential of a situation and manoeuvring to ascertain that the best is made of it for the educational benefit of all present.

To be unskilled in these subtler managerial arts has consequences well known to teachers. Pupils who do not question the teacher's superior knowledge will nevertheless question and probe the authority and confidence used to manage the social situation. The process of negotiating the limits of acceptable behaviour, beyond which punitive sanctions might be employed, is a real part of developing classroom relationships. If it becomes apparent to some pupils that the limits are imprecise or the teacher's negotiating skills are inadequate, it is highly likely that an attempt will be made to exploit these grey areas of the classroom regime.

The presence of West Indian children in the classroom implies an additional range of expressions and behaviours from the minority's cultural repertoire. While a confident teacher may be able to execute his management role in a 'normal' classroom situation, the same teacher may find he is less skilled in the presence of an ethnic minority with distinctive cultural behaviour unknown to him. The effect of the teacher's recognition of these limitations on communications and their implications for teacher attitudes and competence in classrooom control and assessment of pupils are indicated in subsequent sections.

Sources of confusion in teachers' classroom dealings with West Indian pupils

Observations of classroom relations in the Form IV classes at West Midlands School indicated some crucial managerial difficulties for teachers. In situations in which about twelve of the thirty pupils in the class were West Indian (and mostly of Jamaican origin), teachers often seemed unable to establish 'a normal' environment in the classroom. Many of the teachers' difficulties arose from a range of characteristically non-English social meanings in interactions between pupil and teacher and pupil and pupil. These included distinctive physical features, gestures and other codes of communication used by the pupils.

First, in the crucial phase of getting to know a new class, many teachers persistently mistook and confused the identities of their West Indian pupils long after they had learned the names and faces of

English pupils in question. It was also likely to remain in the back of the teacher's mind as an element of uncertainty of judgement about West Indian pupils with whom he (or she) must deal.

Even where identification was no longer a problem, there was another range of potential difficulties. These had to do with elementary expectations about the ways in which body movements and postures might coincide with other sorts of expressive behaviour. It was apparent, for example, when teachers often found that the eye movements of their West Indian pupils did not signal an impending message (for example, of some expected verbal initiative or response). Individuals might look away at those movements when, according to the majority's social etiquette they would not be expected to do so. In this way the expectations of individuals socialised in two cultural settings could give rise both to misunderstandings and heightened ethnic awareness.

Turning the eyes away was observed on many occasions to be made by a West Indian pupil as a sign of deference and respect to a teacher, yet it was received and interpreted by the teacher as an expression of guilt or bad manners. The example shows that such instinctive gestures, learned in early childhood, can upset the rhythm of interaction between individuals and again give rise to a sense of insecurity as each tries to cope with what is for that person an unexpected gesture or posture by the other.

It can be argued that failures of perception at this subtle yet crucial level could and did give rise to a code of classroom communication to which the teacher, though the central and managerial figure in the room, was denied access. Awareness of this development generated anxieties for the teacher, who often became aware that these asymmetrical responses could (and did) give rise to sequences of behaviours that he was not culturally attuned to anticipate. The response to these phenomena might be to become increasingly dominant and strict, or to adopt an easy-going and unflappable posture. Each of these, it is clear, require considerable emotional resources of courage and self-confidence on the part of the teacher.

Thirdly, beyond the reflexive gestures and postures, there were those signs employed by a West Indian pupil to convey specific meaning. The clicking of lips, or pouting them and plucking them with a finger are examples of derogatory expressions which many teachers failed to interpret even when those gestures were directed at them. The impact of the gesture on those children who understood it ranged from disgust to amusement. It could give rise to even more jests of a similarly exclusive kind. Alternatively innocent ethnically-exclusive signs could be interpreted as other than innocent. The lack of skills in understanding and responding subtly to these expressions often proved counter-productive to the main business of the relationship, that is, teaching and learning a particular subject or skill.

Fourthly, there was the use of *patois*, which very few teachers understood. Most teachers appeared to discourage its use, some by the use of strict penalties. It was noteworthy that among the West Indian pupils who were assessed most highly by the staff there were a number of individuals whom the writer never heard to use *patois* in any school circumstances. There could be little doubt that a number of teachers felt threatened by the persistent use of a dialect they could not understand, and that their anxiety expressed itself in their attitudes and behaviour towards those pupils who used it.

These aspects of communication outside the cultural repertoire of the majority clearly provided the basis for obstacles to confident relations between West Indian pupils and their English teachers. Not unnaturally the confusions so generated could be expected to give rise to survival strategies on the part of teachers facing these constraints on their skills of classroom management. At one extreme there were a few teachers who took the strictly authoritarian strategy of dominating absolutely all aspects of classroom social activity (although this was only really possible in shortage-subject lessons where there were few pupils motivated to persistently offensive behaviour *vis-à-vis* the teacher in question and where any offending individual could promptly be removed from the elite set of pupils given access to the shortage subject in question). At the other extreme there were many teachers who got on with their work with the minimum of confrontation over behavioural issues. In these classrooms, the exclusively West Indian forms of behaviour and expression were frequently tolerated by teachers. They were forced to accept certain limitations upon their managerial and teaching roles, and this invariably influenced their attitudes towards those individuals who seemed to be the focus of their difficulties.

Assessment of pupils

Teachers make judgements about their pupils outside as well as inside the classroom. But it would be difficult to argue that such judgements do not reflect classroom experience. Where classroom experience is uncertain and confused, questions naturally arise concerning the reliability of any assessment of individual pupils' abilities and achievements. With this in mind, it is of interest to consider the results of an assessment made of pupils in our age-cohort, then Form IV, when their teachers were asked to rate all their pupils, whatever their ethnic affiliation, on two scales. Analysis of the results of these ratings, one for academic ability and the other for behavioural co-operation, revealed that where West Indian boys and girls were concerned (and not for any other pupil category) there was a very highly significant statistical intercorrelation between the two ratings. In other words, while teachers were in most cases well able to make some discriminating judgements about the abilities and behaviours of English and South Asian pupils, their judgements were rather confused in that there was a strong tendency among them to use the same criteria to judge West Indian children on academic and behavioural terms. From such a confusion it is to be assumed that West Indian pupils were vulnerable to poor assessment of their abilities, and that the assessment given would be most likely to reflect the teachers' subjective involvement with the complex behavioural aspects of classroom relations.

The outworking of the confusion just described was most apparent on the day when pupils were allocated to the three CSE courses at the beginning of their fourth year. Each boy or girl was put into either the top stream (or full CSE course), the middle stream (or partial CSE course), or the bottom stream (the remnant considered too poor to sit the CSE examinations in any subject). Political and professional prudence on the part of the headmaster saw to it that the major ethnic categories of the pupil population were more or less proportionately represented in both the top and bottom streams. In the middle stream the number of West Indian pupils, particularly of West Indian boys, was highly disproportionate to their presence in the age grade as a whole. In that stream, twenty out of twenty-five pupils were West Indian, and it is possible that this ethnic composition reflects the problematic nature of teachers' confused social and academic judgements of their West Indian pupils. One West Indian boy commented upon his allocation to the middle stream: 'Sir, we're here because we're pretty'. The comment could well have been a telling one. Later that day, Form IV's West Indian boys, particularly those of the two lower streams, were responsible for a trail of havoc as they left for home: car tyres were slashed, fire-alarm bells set off, waste-bins upturned and windows broken.

Throughout their two final years at school, West Indian pupils continued to experience difficulties in meeting their own aspirations. On the one hand their frustration was expressed by a large number of drop-outs among them; on the other hand, those who remained enjoyed such low prestige with their teachers, that they were effectively waiting out their time in school with no worthwhile academic achievements within their grasp (the demoralising process described by Clark as 'cooling out', Clark, 1962). The average level of results obtained by West Indian boys in the final examinations were dramatically lower than for any other pupil category. Their average result of two grade 5 CSE passes each was so poor as to have little more than token value. In comparison West Indian girls did three times better than this (which was about average for pupils in the age grade as a whole).

These results for West Indian pupils are particularly poignant when it is realised that the boys' abilities, as measured on scores obtained on intelligence tests, were superior to those of the girls of their own ethnic set. The diametrically opposed trends of school achievements and intelligence ratings could only be explained for West Indian boys and girls in terms of an analysis of their approach to schoolwork and their teachers' interactions with them. To complete our analysis along these lines, it is necessary to consider the pupils' own perspectives on their secondary school experience at West Midland School.

Pupil perception and support

Certain marked attitudes and developments were noted among West Indian pupils. First, West Indian girls made increasing efforts to minimise social misunderstandings and maximise co-operating with their teachers. However, the pattern of West Indian boys' attitudes appeared to run in the converse direction. Secondly, it appeared that the ethnically distinctive social and cultural behaviours and activities were, in the case of the West Midland School, predominantly Jamaican. As children of Jamaican origin formed a numerical majority there was therefore much greater chance that the West Indian pupils who formed the focus of teachers' classroom difficulties would be Jamaican rather than non-Jamaican. There was also greater opportunity for these youngsters to maintain and develop Jamaican cultural values and styles. Thirdly, in this situation one could rightly deduce that boys from Jamaican home backgrounds were particularly likely to come into collision with their teachers. These boys were the chief protagonists of a set of vigorous and stimulating social and cultural activities.

The behavioural attitudes of the West Indian girls in Form IV must be seen as one stage in their development throughout their secondary school career. In the junior classes these girls had been more the focus of teachers' classroom difficulties than the boys. Many teachers explained the high levels of excitability and even physical violence among these girls in terms of the intense peer competition into which they moved with the onset of puberty and adolescence. However these emotional strains did not appear to persist much into adolescence, possibly due to the interest taken in them by their mother and by other members of the family at home. The evidence here suggests that girls were pressured to recognise that the supportive adults at home provided much greater long-term security for them as individuals and as potential mothers. They understood that their best contribution to that supportive unit was to obtain the best economic and social standing which they could manage. In return, the supportive unit could be guaranteed to provide protection in the child-bearing years and, later on give the matriarchal prestige of older women in many West Indian households. The West Indian girls in Form IV were thus conformists to established family and social norms, conserving and building upon the economic and social assets to which they had access. They were more concerned with longer-term personal security than shorter-term social prestige and popularity (see Weinreich, this volume).

By contrast, the West Indian boys whose cases were considered displayed increasingly ambivalent and even hostile attitudes towards their teachers and their school experience in general. These developments coincided in many instances with difficult relations with parents. Some had even been thrown out of the household and were compelled to seek lodgings either with relatives, older peers living in flats or bed-sitters, or in a local shelter run by community workers. As they advanced into adolescence, almost all West Indian boys gave themselves energetically to peer activities and in so doing often isolated themselves even more from both parents and teachers. Their strong and more enduring ties were largely with other West Indian boys and solidarity and distinctiveness was expressed symbolically in styles of dress, musical tastes, recreational interests, physical competitiveness, joking relationships, etc. Only a few individuals opted out of this pattern and in each case they were boys who enjoyed a more positive rapport with either parents or teachers (or both). This small minority found a social niche for themselves in the comparatively rare cases of cross-ethnic friendships with English or South Asian boys, a development approved by their teachers.

The general trend of peer pressure, however, led most West Indian boys to exploit every social opportunity to gain prestige with their ethnic peers (see Weinreich, this volume). Their concern was most clearly played out in the social and recreational activities associated with school life, but there could be no doubt that it also interfered with what might otherwise have been normal classroom relations. As has been indicated previously, many classroom situations were ripe for manipulation in this kind of way because of the apparent limitations in the cultural competences of many teachers to perceive and interpret distinctive ethnic behaviour and expressions. As a result, though many of these boys persisted in the belief that they were able to do well at school, they found themselves to be held in poor esteem by their teachers. Here were all the ingredients for mutual suspicion and disapproval. Teachers were seen to act harshly, even vindictively, in matters of social punishments and academic grades. Ethnic peer solidarity, in the face of even further isolation and apparent hostility, was for many boys the only supportive resource.

The second general development in attitudes and loyalties among West Indian pupils at the West Midlands School was due to the influence of Jamaican cultural values and styles. The majority of those boys and girls came from rural Jamaica and shared a common *patois*, and in some cases had common recollections of life 'back home'. By contrast, the children whose families had come from the smaller British Caribbean islands did not share common backgrounds, and often felt themselves to be very different from the Jamaicans. In terms of attitudes towards the English majority in general, and towards teachers in particular, there was undoubtedly some difference. Although not all teachers readily recognised the different cultural backgrounds of their West Indian pupils, there was a strong tendency for non-Jamaican pupils to enjoy more positive relations with teachers compared to Jamaican pupils. One may only speculate that the reasons for this were partly linguistic (these pupils would be less likely to employ the predominantly Jamaican *patois*) and partly social (being less inclined to identify with predominantly Jamaican behaviour and groupings).

The sensitivity of West Indian pupils to the ethnic differences between themselves influenced their social behaviour. These subtler ethnic differences were reflected in the teachers' assessments and the pupils final examination results. The development of these patterns does not imply that they could be expected to occur in other institutional circumstances where the ethnic composition of the pupil population and the personalities of the pupils is different. However, in the specific circumstances of this study, there was a strong tendency for the critical social and educational difficulties outlined to be associated with West Indian boys from Jamaican home backgrounds, and to a lesser extent with other West Indian pupils.

Conclusion

This case study suggests that West Indian pupils were exposed to considerable personal insecurities and difficulties which arose from their teachers' confusion. Pupils turned to ethnic sources of support; for the girls these were usually within the household and family, while for the boys they lay in peer relationships. For the girls, these resources contributed to levels of school achievement which their teachers tended not to anticipate. The boys' resort to stronger peer alliances seemed to serve mainly to discredit them socially and academically in the eyes of their teachers.

The strain and stress experienced by West Indian minority pupils and their English majority teachers in their classroom dealings with one another offers a valuable explanation of the levels of school achievement attained by these pupils. The strain in classroom relations appeared more readily to be explained in terms of teachers' confusions of social judgement due to their lack of competence in the cultural repertoire of West Indian pupils than in terms of any consistent conspiracy on the part of such teachers. The reasons for their deficient knowledge and skill in this area are readily apparent if the general historical and social experience of teachers over the past twenty-five years is remembered. It is one in which the emphasis has been placed upon their status as teachers and their membership of the dominant ethnic category, defining the rules and expectations of the classroom in terms of assimilation to the wider society.

Classroom teaching in these circumstances must bring teachers increasingly into conflict with their West Indian minority pupils. The alleviation of these difficulties must be largely in the hands of teachers prepared to develop their cultural skills to interact competently with West Indian minority pupils. It is the task of the policy-makers to create the conditions in institutions and appropriate training to induce teachers to develop that competence. At its core, the change in educational policy required must acknowledge the legitimacy of cultural forms generated outside the ethnic majority's cultural setting. It must be a pluralist policy. The alternative is ethnic confrontation in which educators become oppressors.

7

Other statutory services besides the educational system are constrained by a philosophy and code of practice which, in certain important respects, are not appropriate to sections of our population. Many workers in the social and medical services have had little training for work with ethnic minorities and are now increasingly aware of the need for an understanding of their clients' culture and conditions of life. This paper asks the fundamental question of how a whole professional system can adjust to the realities of working in a multi-cultural society, and reminds us that many of the questions have in fact been asked before in relation to class and cultural differences of the indigenous population.

The question points to the need for information about ethnic minorities, but also to the need to assess the culturally specific values which underlie the everyday assumptions and practices of professional social workers. Only in the light of this, can the relevant training be given and an effective service be provided. The paper outlines the major areas in which the 'traditional' view of things needs to be reassessed and begins to indicate the practices and provisions which may need to be introduced to provide an effective service – one which is complementary to supportive systems within the minority communities. We are reminded that all these decisions have political implications and thus demand the consideration of the motives and objectives of all participants.

Ethnic Minorities and the Social Services

What type of service?

Roger Ballard

Although there are now substantial Asian and West Indian settlements in most major British cities, the issues which their presence raises for the social services are still being approached with uncertainty. The limited literature that is available generally looks at members of these groups as 'immigrants' (see, for example, Fitzherbert, 1967; Cheetham, 1972; Triseliotis, 1972; Jones, 1976). Their cultural and social backgrounds are described, as are their reasons for migrating to Britain, and the problems that they have in adjusting to their new environment. It is almost always assumed, explicitly or implicitly, that the cultural distinctiveness of members of minority groups will gradually fade, so that the behaviour of their children will, for instance, closely resemble that of the remainder of the population. However, it is now becoming increasingly evident that whatever earlier commentators may have assumed, a straightforward process of assimilation is not taking place. The 'immigrant' minorities are sustaining culturally distinctive patterns of social relations, which are a product of their experiences in Britain, quite as much as of their roots overseas. The central aim of this paper is to consider the problems which the presence of relatively permanent ethnic collectivities pose for practitioners, institutions and ideologies currently established in the whole field of the social services. There is at present very little, and often nothing at all, in the training of practitioners in the social services – among whom should be included doctors, psychiatrists and health visitors as well as the broad range of social workers and probation officers – which will prepare them for working with members of ethnic minority groups. Many practitioners in inner

city areas are becoming increasingly perplexed as they try to understand the culturally specific aspects of their clients' behaviour. Some
have begun to acquire considerable knowledge and expertise as the
outcome of practical experience. Yet there must be doubt about the
quality of service which such *ad hoc* experts are able to provide, not
only because their numbers are small, but also because their specialism – if indeed it is recognised as such – is rarely regarded as
important, and so they very often receive little institutional support
and encouragement.

   This paper has not been written as the outcome of normal experience in social work. It stems mainly from observations made during
an anthropological study of the Sikh community in Leeds in which the
focus was on regularities within the community rather than upon
deviance and personal problems. The researchers did, however,
become involved in a number of cases where individuals faced personal and family difficulties, and it soon emerged that the established
agencies were often ill-equipped either to understand the real nature
of the problems, or to offer advice and assistance which was in any
way appropriate to their solution.[1] The researchers also found themselves drawn into a very small number of extremely complicated cases
where they acted as intermediaries with professional agencies. It has
unfortunately not been possible to illustrate the arguments presented
here with case studies of these experiences, partly because of lack of
space, but more particularly because of problems of confidentiality
and the difficulty of making an objective commentary on events in
which the writer has been personally involved.[2]

   Problems concerning the needs of ethnic minorities are now arising
in all branches of the social services. Even the simplest of them may
have complex ramifications. For example, how should a doctor's
receptionist who finds her files full of cards for Mr Singhs and Mrs
Begums set about reorganising her filing system? Should South Asian
menus be offered in hospitals with significant numbers of Indian,
Pakistani and Bangladeshi patients? Even if this is accepted in principle, it is not easy to identify a diet which would be acceptable to
Hindus, Moslems and Sikhs. Do elderly South Asians, or South Asian
girls who have run away from home, need the same kind of provisions
as those available to the majority population, or do they have special
needs? Should the state respond to those special needs or is it a
voluntary matter? How far should social workers take minority patterns of family organisation into account in the course of case work?

How far are a psychiatrist's conventional diagnostic categories relevant when dealing with South Asian patients who claim to be possessed by spirits or to be victims of mystical poisoning?

The fact that members of ethnic minorities organise their lives in culturally distinctive ways must necessarily cause problems for practitioners who come into contact with a new group for the first time. Whether they realise it or not, they step, like Alice, into an unfamiliar world. Once across the ethnic boundary – which may, confusingly, be shifting and invisible – they can never be quite sure whether things really mean what they seem to, or rather what they would have done had the rules of the more normal and familiar world continued to apply. Indeed in the absence of a knowledge of the distinctive internal ethnic rules and logics, it may become impossible to tell whether any item of behaviour is normal or aberrant. The misinterpretations which can so easily arise in such situations may have very unfortunate consequences. When minority cultural patterns do not mesh with professional practices and institutional structures which have been generated in another cultural setting, it is easy to lose sight of the real problems. It is easy to slip, instead, into regarding distinctive minority cultural patterns themselves as being problematic and pathological (see Valentine, 1968). The central argument of this paper is, on the contrary, that the culturally specific practices of the minorities, which are currently frequently seen as confusing and problematic liabilities, could more usefully be understood as coherent systems. Properly tapped they might even become potentially valuable resources for social services agencies. The suggestion is therefore not only that the provision of ethnically sensitive services should be a normal part of good professional practice, but also that such an approach might throw a new, and more positive, light on much that currently appears problematic.

The argument is put forward particularly with reference to migrants of South Asian origin, but it is intended to be exploratory rather than definitive. It is hoped, however, that it may be useful in drawing together some questions which practitioners in a range of professions are currently finding problematic, and that it may also define some areas for debate in this complicated field. It is also worth emphasising at the outset that a concern with cultural factors does not lead simply to a discussion of the ways in which existing practices could be extended or modified for the new ethnic minorities alone. When the arguments are pursued they inevitably lead back to a consideration of the culturally specific values which underlie every-day professional assumptions and practices. It could be that many of the arguments presented here in connection with ethnic minorities could be replicated with respect to class and regional differences within what will be described here, simply for the sake of convenience, as the ethnic majority.

Family relationships in their cultural setting

Many of the difficulties which bring individuals into contact with the social services will not be cultural at all, at least in origin. Members of ethnic minorities, just like anyone else, may fall ill or become de-pressed, become the sole adult responsible for a family, lose control over their children, or run into problems over money, housing or employment. However, although such physical and material prob-lems may be universal, they do arise within particular cultural set-tings. They therefore present themselves in different ways and with varying frequency in each ethnic group. The precise cultural context may make the same problem more or less intense, and it needs to be taken into account if meaningful professional assistance is to be given. In a poly-cultural situation it is essential to start with an open mind. Those working with ethnic minorities can expect to find some familiar problems largely absent, some emerging in novel ways and others of a kind which they have never met before.

For most practitioners in the social services the most important cultural differences are those which have a bearing on the personal and above all on the familial life of the individual. While it is obvious that South Asians, Chinese, Cypriots, West Africans, West Indians and many other groups all organise their families in very different ways, inadequate information can lead to major misunderstandings. In the case of West Indian families, for example, it is all too easy to misinterpret a loosely structured matrifocal family group as necessar-ily being problematic. Being an unmarried mother may not be nearly as difficult as it might be in another cultural setting. In many parts of the West Indies for example, the cultural expectation is for grand-mothers to play an important part in bringing up their grandchildren. Girls may become mothers but do not necessarily marry the father of their child and unmarried fathers may still acknowledge the paternity of their children. In Britain therefore it might be more appropriate to provide greater facilities for the proper exercise of grandmotherhood than to try to counsel marriage or abortion. South Asian family life, in contrast, is often believed to be too constricting. If an Indian or Pakistani woman is in conflict with her parents or husband, an outsider may assume that the subordinate role which South Asian women are expected to play towards their fathers and husbands, or the institution of the arranged marriage, is at the root of the problem. Such an interpretation might be partially correct, but the woman would be unlikely to be seeking to alter her situation fundamentally. To do so would be to reject a major part of the cultural values of her own ethnic group. Her complaint is, in practice, much more likely to be about the particular behaviour of her own husband or father, measured not in terms of majority standards, but of those of her own group. It is important that solutions should be sought within the particular cultural context, that is the values in terms of which people organise their own lives. Solutions which, whether intentionally or not, have the effect of ignoring or condemning those values are likely to be unacceptable to the recipients.

In poly-ethnic situations, professional agencies need to have a sense of cultural relativity, so that the activities of one group are not judged by the standards of another. Such a perspective makes it possible to avoid making judgements about the relative merits of different cultural systems. It prompts a realisation that cultures must be seen as systematic totalities and that an attempt to evaluate single elements in isolation is meaningless. For instance, the possibility of parents arranging their children's marriages is inconceivable in the contemporary British cultural context, because among other things it would run quite counter to the way in which the rest of an individual's family life is organised. For South Asians, the reverse is largely true. Not to have an arranged marriage runs against the whole ethos of family organisation. Finally, a sense of cultural relativity can bring a realisation that most things cut both ways. The tightly organised Asian family may limit individual freedom, but because loyalty to the group is put before personal self-interest, no one need feel insecure. Who can judge whether liberty or security should be regarded as the higher value, or what emphasis should be given to each? Quite obviously the members of the minority should, and in any case will, choose the values which they wish to follow.

Such an outlook should not, however, be taken to be one of conservatism. If it is assumed that cultural systems are by their very nature fixed and static, it seems to follow that cultural autonomy can be sustained only if each is preserved in absolute purity. But this is to misunderstand the nature of culture. All cultures necessarily have a strong element of continuity, for this alone allows the genesis of mutual understanding between individuals. Nevertheless, all groups, all generations and indeed all individuals adapt, change and modify the culture, or cultures, to which they have been exposed in response to the particular circumstances in which they find themselves. However, there is nothing straightforward about the direction of such changes. It has been widely assumed that the members of ethnic minorities would eventually become culturally identical with the majority: a process of assimilation. Although some cultural changes in a 'British' direction can certainly be identified in all the minorities, by no means all change is in this direction. Indeed it is becoming increasingly evident that distinct and separate patterns of behaviour are being sustained by the second generation in most minority groups. The reasons for this have been discussed in detail elsewhere (see C. Ballard and Driver in this volume, and Roger and Catherine Ballard, 1977). Essentially the maintenance of ethnic distinctiveness is the outcome of the strength of childhood socialisation, of interaction with peers, and of a reaction to hostility and misunderstanding from the majority.

Young people, but particularly those from minority groups, are likely to display a range of cultural competences (Goodenough, 1971) which give them the ability to act and react in an appropriate manner in a range of different settings. Thus, for instance, young Asians can be observed moving without difficulty from the 'traditional' world of the *Gurdwara* to the 'Western' world of school and work, and behaving in ways different again within their own friendship groups. This fact that a person can operate competently within a particular cultural setting should not be taken as evidence that he cannot, or would not wish to, operate in another. Nor can it be predicted whether one particular cultural system will prove more viable than another. The networks of relationships established among themselves by members of the younger generation are likely to be based on a reinterpretation of values, styles and skills drawn from a wide range of sources, or even invented from scratch. However derivative, degenerate or problematic such cultural systems may seem to others, they are best understood as vigorous, vital and inherently autonomous phenomena. Those who participate in them are constantly negotiating and inventing new understandings, new patterns of relationships and hence new cultures as they go along. Such processes of change among young people are clearly far less straightforward than the commonly used concepts of assimilation and culture conflict seem to suggest.

Any attempt to deal with the theoretical roots of the issues of cultural relativity and change necessarily generates a good deal of rather abstract argument. Nevertheless it needs to be stressed that the availability of a limited amount of relatively simple information, if effectively presented, could radically improve the effectiveness of practitioners working with ethnic minority groups. Greater knowledge and sensitivity on their part might also lead to patients and clients revealing to practitioners a much greater proportion of their problems as they themselves conceived them. During the course of field-work it became evident that many people had learned only to present a fraction of their real concerns, for they did not *expect* outsiders to have any understanding of, or sympathy with, their own customs and beliefs. Indeed a frequent strategy was to present problems in a way which, they hoped, would make sense in terms of majority assumptions.

Community structure and its implications

So far differences in family and kinship structures have been used in order to illustrate some of the ways in which confusion and misunderstandings may arise, but there are two further spheres of differences which are worth examining in some detail, particularly with respect to South Asian groups. They are first, the question of communal organisation, and secondly, that of theories of causation. Although there are broad similarities between people from all parts of the Indian sub-continent, there are nevertheless distinct differences between them. There is certainly no such thing as a single coherent South Asian community in Britain. Even those people who do share a common religion and region of origin, such as Mirpuri Moslems or Punjabi Sikhs, do not necessarily form a single coherent community when they are settled in a British city. (For a detailed discussion see Saifullah Khan, 1976c.) There are close and tight-knit social aggregations, but these tend to be much smaller in scale, usually being focused on a particular village, kinship or caste group. It is the kinship group (variously described in different dialects, but the term *biraderi* is widely used) which is the primary arena for social interaction for most South Asian migrants. It is to their kinsmen that they look for support in times of trouble, it is among their kinsmen that they compete for and dispute about honour and prestige, *izzat*, and it is from their kinsmen that they fear sanctions (the worst of which is expulsion) if they behave in a manner which is considered to be deviant. The *biraderi*, or its equivalent, is a corporate group, whose members expect mutual assistance. They also expect to sort out each other's troubles, not least because if those troubles were to become public – to the British, but particularly to their compatriots – the *izzat* of the group as a whole would be affected. Expulsion restores the honour of the remainder of the group, but it also leaves the expelled person without communal attachment, a highly unattractive fate in Asian terms.

The strength of family ties in South Asian cultures are well known and have already been stressed, but one often imperfectly understood consequence of this is that the main communal groupings are best seen as being composed not so much of individuals, but of families, each of which is a little community in itself. One result of this is that disputes between individuals invariably intimately involve other members of the family. In addition, a whole series of people, more distant relatives, are likely to feel that they have an interest in the outcome of the dispute: their *izzat* might possibly also be at stake. Social workers who find themselves dealing with personal disputes thus need to recognise that they have to deal with a much wider body of people than they would normally expect. This may sometimes be a frustrating and time-consuming experience, but on the other hand, if it proves possible to move with, rather than against, traditional procedures then some things may go more smoothly than expected. In a world of corporate groups, be they families or *biraderis*, the idea of the broker or go-between, whose task it is to find some sort of mutually acceptable compromise, is well established.

The corporate organisations of Asian communities provide a great deal of support for their members, and indeed ever since the first Asian settlers arrived in Britain they have been the essence of communal organisation. However, as was mentioned earlier, such tight-knit organisations are not without disadvantages, for they are both supportive and constricting (see Saifullah Khan, this volume). Individuals who find their way to professional practitioners in the social services are likely to be those for whom these internal mechanisms of support have failed to operate, or who feel, at least at that moment, that communal entanglement is oppressive. But such dissatisfaction should not necessarily be taken as a wish to escape the minority ethnic world altogether, and it is also obviously profoundly mistaken to assume that anglicisation and liberation are the same thing. Are British cultural conventions really so satisfactory? It is easy to slip away from a consideration of an individual's problems within his own personal context, and to make simplistic value judgements about the cultural system in terms of which that context is organised.

All professional theories and practices have of course been generated within a particular cultural context, and they therefore necessarily embody a complex scheme of cultural values. It seems clear, however, that these values are relatively rarely explicitly spelled out, and even less rarely considered in relation to the ways in which the recipients of those practices actually organise their lives. Such an argument can evidently be applied not only with respect to the ethnic minorities, but also to the various culturally distinct groups amongst the ethnic majority. Despite the fact that there are a wide (and often contradictory) range of schools of thought about how social workers can most usefully go about their task – as case workers, community workers or as promoters of self-help or welfare rights – almost all seem to underpin their theory with an ideology which stresses the necessity and values of individual freedom and self-determination. Such ideological foundations may be appropriate when dealing with members of the majority, who do largely live in a world of individuals, and who have certainly been socialised into individualistic ideologies. However, they may be a very poor starting point when dealing with corporately organised communities where obligation to others is always expected to over-ride personal self-interest. Paradoxically, the more South Asians move towards the values enshrined in social work theory, the more they may find themselves in need of social workers.

Misfortune and theories of causation

Ethnic minorities do not just differ from familiar majority patterns in a few details, but rather in the whole system of values and assumptions which they use to order the world in which they live. This applies not only at the levels of family, kinship and community, but also to the way in which the root causes of personal difficulties are conceptualised. Apart from taking straightfoward action to deal with an immediate problem, be it ill-health, an accident, financial misfortune or a breakdown in personal relationships, most people of South Asian origin are very concerned with the question of why it is that a particular family or person should have been afflicted at that particular time. There is a strong belief that all events have a place within a supernatural logic. The precise concepts in terms of which this is structured vary between different religious groups, but the forces which are believed to be important include a person's *karma*, that is the consequence of his activities in previous lives, his *kismet* or fate, the influence of God, minor deities and spirits of various kinds, of the stars, and also of the magical activities of other people. In situations of adversity many people may therefore seek the guidance of a spiritual adviser to identify the source of the affliction, and above all in order that they may take action, usually of a mystical kind, to counteract its influence. If illness is the problem, such steps may be taken in parallel to consultations with a physician, on the logically unassailable grounds that although drugs and medicines may relieve the immediate symptons, they can do nothing to counter the malevolent mystical forces which caused misfortune to strike and which, if left untreated, would result in the future eruption of some new affliction.

To those who have been trained and socialised in the rational and secular traditions of modern European society, such beliefs are likely to be seen as irrelevances which prevent their South Asian clients from gaining an accurate perception of their troubles. But are these ideas about supernatural powers as alien or as unhelpful as they seem at first sight? In the British cultural context, most popular newspapers and magazines print columns of astrological predictions, evidently in response to popular demand. Although individuals may be rather shamefaced when pressed about superstition, 'luck', 'fate' and 'good fortune' are thoroughly familiar concepts. Those who employ them are a much larger number than the minority who are regular churchgoers, but it is worth remembering that religious institutions still do provide support, fellowship and guidance for their congregations, as well as a set of causal explanations of the same general kind as those which have just been outlined. Prayer and confession may simply be more familiar ideas than meditation and the ritual propitiation of spirits.

It is easy for an observer who stands outside a system of belief to dismiss its ideas as misguided. Yet such ideas form coherent systems which are such a central part of the cultural traditions of South Asian settlers that many aspects of their lives cannot be understood without reference to them. In so far as a person's state of mind may have a major influence on his physical and mental well-being, and certainly upon his speed of recovery after an illness or emotional disturbance, the way in which he conceptualises his world is of undeniable importance. Religious and 'magical' remedies may indeed be effective because they provide uniquely meaningful explanations, and also powerfully reinforce confidence. However, in a situation where magico-religious beliefs are pervasive, the 'rational' and the 'magical', the physical and the mental, are not always so easily separable. Very often allegations about supernatural processes may be a means of making statements about real social relationships. However, in the absence of an understanding of the code, such communications may seem bizarre and deluded, evidence perhaps of schizophrenia. For example, in the South Asian cultural code, a wife's preparation and serving of food for her husband is one of her foremost public duties, and likewise, a husband demonstrates the unity of their marriage by eating the food served. If a woman fails to provide food for her husband, or if the husband fails to eat the food provided, it can be taken that, at the very least, some aspect of the spouse's behaviour is being objected to. From the husband's side, an additional twist may be given by his arguing that he cannot eat the food offered to him, because it has been 'poisoned'. Quite what the poison is or whether it is there at all is beside the point. By making this allegation, the husband suggests that his wife has totally inverted her obligations to him, and that she therefore does not, at least for the while, deserve to be regarded as his wife. In Asian families, tensions and conflicts are frequently articulated in terms of such veiled shafts of accusation and counter-accusation. Outsiders who lack the necessary cultural competence may not only be baffled by what they hear, but may proceed to struggle to quite inaccurate conclusions about what is happening. It is much easier to diagnose schizophrenia than to try to come to terms with the culturally-specific symbolic system within which the patient is expressing himself (see Rack, this volume).

The provision of more effective services

In the space available it has only been possible to sketch out the dimensions of a few of the novel problems which members of ethnic minorities may present to the social services. A great deal of research still needs to be done on the actual content of interactions between social workers and their ethnic minority clients. The paper has been written as a result of experience with South Asians, and a parallel, but different, set of arguments could be presented for every one of the minorities, including the West Indians, West Africans, Yemenis, Chinese, Cypriot, Gypsy and even the Irish communities in Britain. Given the limitations of this paper and also the fact that information on the values and internal structures of the minorities is still in very short supply, it would be presumptuous, as well as premature, to try to lay down detailed prescriptions as to how more ethnically sensitive services might be provided. Nevertheless, it is possible to suggest some broad indications of the form which a more appropriate professional response might take.

Cultural considerations will obviously be of greater importance in some kinds of situations than in others. In those cases which involve a client's most immediate personal and familial world, an extensive knowledge of the appropriate cultural codes and structures will almost certainly be a prerequisite for understanding what is at issue and providing assistance in moving towards an effective solution. In such cases, some kind of ethnic specialisation by practitioners would seem to be unavoidable. However, it needs to be stressed that the majority of cases where members of the ethnic minorities come into contact with the social services – for instance as patients in hospital, as mothers needing home helps, as potential adoptive parents, as offenders on probation, or as children being examined by health visitors – the question of cultural differences is likely to be peripheral to the service being provided. Yet the fact that they are peripheral does not mean that they are professionally irrelevant, not least because no one can be understood outside his cultural context.

When a professional, whether a social worker, a psychiatrist, a health visitor, a teacher or a probation officer shares the same, or at least a similar, social and cultural background with his client, a great deal can be, or at least usually is, taken for granted. If this is so, then it follows that a great deal of the analysis and theoretical assumptions, as well as the goals, support and advice preferred by professionals in the established social services actually consists of problem-solving within the specific but unacknowledged arena of British cultural values. When clients are drawn from ethnic minorities, the existence of such a shared cultural and linguistic code evidently cannot be taken for granted, but reactions to this situation vary enormously, both between individuals and professions. Some practitioners blithely manage to ignore all differences, making statements such as 'I treat everyone as an individual regardless of their background'. Such statements often mask a kind of cultural imperialism, where it is the clients who are expected to make all the adaptations, and where it is they who are regarded as being responsible for their own misfortunes if they fail to do so. Nevertheless, a substantial number of professionals are now coming to feel that they should take the cultural values of the minorities more seriously (see Rack, this volume, for detailed examples). They often find to their regret, however, that they lack training, knowledge and experience which might give them a greater understanding of the significance and purpose of their client's beliefs and actions. Practitioners with heavy case loads are unlikely to find much time to ponder such questions as to whether what they see as problematic also seems problematic to their minority clients, or whether this is merely a mirage created by their own limited knowledge. Even the most sympathetic may find themselves taking hasty and ill-considered decisions, putting the case aside to deal with more straightforward but equally pressing matters. Any practitioner who does not have a working knowledge of the way in which his clients order, or seek to order, their social worlds, the goals they are attempting to achieve, the style of behaviour they habitually adopt, and the kinds of material, cultural and social constraints under which they are operating must necessarily be professionally handicapped.

Given the relatively shallow time depth of most minority settlements in Britain it is not suprising that knowledge of the extent and content of ethnic diversity is extremely limited in the majority population. Yet it would seem to be highly desirable that this deficiency should be made good, and that all professional training courses should give some guidance as to how to develop the appropriate skills and sensitivities for working with ethnic minorities. It should also be stressed again that these issues do not arise solely with respect to ethnic minorities. In so far as most professionals are middle class in their own life-style and values, while many of their clients are working class, rather similar problems may arise.

Much needs to be done to increase the level of awareness of these issues among practitioners, but it would be naive to suggest that this could be done simply at the level of initial training courses, or that such courses could provide students with all they need to know. The provision of a great deal more information to those already in practice in those areas where there are substantial minority communities is also required. Much thought also needs to be given to the way in which that information should best be presented in order to improve their professional and cultural competence, and also to the way in which the experience of those practitioners who have already developed such competence could be more effectively drawn upon.

The extent to which practitioners will need to develop such new competences would depend very much on the nature of their clientele, but nevertheless there will always be cases where the cultural complexities are so great that only a person with very extensive knowledge is likely to be able to get to the roots of the matter. In such circumstances there might be no alternative but the provision of some kind of specialist ethnic service. To some extent such a service does already exist, in that clients of non-European origin are often passed to the nearest non-European social worker on the grounds that they are bound to understand one another better. This is by no means necessarily the case, as when a West Indian is sent to an Asian probation officer, or a Punjabi of peasant origin is sent to a psychiatrist from an affluent urban family in South India. In such situations it may also come about that complex cases are referred to practitioners of junior status, and that proper supervision and discussion of their work may never take place. Many professionals drawn from the minorities resent being treated as ethnic specialists, feeling that they are being pushed into a kind of ghetto, dealing with second-class cases in a backwater, from which they believe, probably rightly, that they would have great difficulty in achieving promotion to more senior posts. As a result many, if not most, completely avoid any kind of ethnic specialisation, and instead conform as closely as possible to the styles and practices appropriate to the majority. A radical re-evaluation of the significance, status and importance of work with ethnic minorities is urgently needed, as is a recognition that such work may raise some challenging and disturbing questions. Were this to occur, many more practitioners from the minorities might willingly choose to become specialists in this area, where they would obviously find themselves at a great advantage over their colleagues of majority extraction. Such specialisation, whether at the level of individual practitioners or the establishment of formal institutional structures (for example, a refuge for Asian women), is unlikely to be achieved without considerable difficulty. Specialisation of this type would almost certainly be opposed by the established members of the professions who often hold the apparently universalistic, but in fact profoundly ethnocentric view that 'we treat individuals with problems. Their class, colour, religion and culture are quite immaterial.' Furthermore, in the context of public discussion, the provision of differential services for the minorities is frequently regarded as extra, additional and specially favourable treatment, and hence condemned as unfair and unacceptable to the majority (see CRC, 1977). Some ethnic minorities are also racial minorities against whom there is a great deal of hostility and bitter feelings, particularly when they are seen as competitors for scarce resources.

It is of course partly as a consequence of this reaction from the majority that the minorities have organised themselves ethnically. They have utilised as resources the knowledge, skills and values which they brought with them from their homelands to construct institutions of mutual support, a private system of social services as it were, which has enabled them to survive and sometimes to prosper in alien and often hostile surroundings. Much work has yet to be done on identifying the existing modes of communal support, and on seeking viable ways of strengthening them, instead of trying to replace them. The problems arising from such strategies should not, however, be underestimated. Above all they may raise complex questions about the cultural grounding of majority professional practices which are normally regarded as 'scientific' and universalistic.

Some of these questions can be clearly illustrated in the field of medicine. There are now, for instance, an increasing number of *hakims* and *vaids* in practice in Britain. These are physicians who respectively utilise the *unnani* and *ayurvedic* systems of medicine, diagnosing and treating their patients accordingly. They rely on a fairly powerful pharmacopoeia, which, placed alongside their understanding of their patients' social and psychological condition, often allows them to achieve positive therapeutic results. Many South Asians in Britain consult such physicians for certain conditions, although almost all consult doctors trained in 'modern' or allopathic medicine as well (Mohammed Aslam: personal communication). However, many South Asians feel that a *hakim* or a *vaid* is likely to respond to them much more sympathetically than do most allopathic doctors (including those of South Asian origin) and believe that their remedies are, at least for certain conditions, more efficacious.

The very existence of *unnani* and *ayurvedic* physicians with flourishing practices demonstrates that they are responding effectively to at least part of a need, even if most allopathic doctors tend to be sceptical of their professional competence. *Vaids* and *hakims* are clear examples of internal modes of communal support, yet it can hardly be doubted that the established medical organisations in Britain would oppose any move to give public recognition and support to such physicians. Indeed it is most likely that, if they were more widely known about, arguments would be advanced to the effect that such 'quacks' and 'charlatans' are dangerous meddlers who should be suppressed as soon as possible.

Nevertheless it is evidently important that the scientific and the cultural elements in such judgements should be separated, and that it should not be supposed that allopathic physicians' medical practices are always necessarily superior to those of others. The issues here are very complex. Just how great is the potential of the *ayurvedic* and *unnani* pharmacopoeia? How effectively is it actually deployed? Is allopathic medicine, given the trenchant criticisms of Illich (1975) really as safe as it is regularly assumed to be? Non-western medicine may lack antibiotics and surgery, but are there *no* conditions for which its remedies are at least on a par with, if not superior to, those of allopathy? Could it be that *hakims* and *vaids* are sometimes able to achieve superior results because they take it for granted that their patients' health is the outcome of the simultaneous operation of physiological, psychological and sociological processes? Finally, and most fundamentally, can illness, good health, therapy, and hence the very practice of medicine itself be considered in isolation from its cultural context?

The challenge here, which applies to a whole series of fields besides medicine, is one of establishing communication and understanding at a whole range of levels: between doctors and patients, between social workers and their clients, and between all those who provide personal social services, whatever the professional and cultural provenance of their therapeutic models. The barriers can only be broken down if all the various parties agree to attempt to understand what others are saying and doing, however absurd and untenable this may seem to them at first sight. Too often this does not occur, for it is all too easy to slip into a perception of the cultural worlds of others as an irrational product of sheer ignorance. Action based on such premises does no more than demonstrate the social power of the practitioner.

Conclusion

The core of the argument which has been presented here is that if relevant, effective and universal social services are to be provided in an ethnically diverse society, differential provisions which respond to that diversity must be made. The extent of the differentiation that is desirable will depend on the circumstances, but it will tend to grow more necessary the more closely domestic and personal matters are involved. In no circumstances is the fact of ethnic diversity likely to be of no relevance at all. It is clear, however, that regular provision of ethnically sensitive services is not likely to be a speedy or straightforward achievement. Lack of information, lack of appropriately trained personnel, and the lack of clearly thought out models of what an ethnically grounded response should actually be are some of the problems that have already been outlined. However, it is important to remember that all these issues have a political dimension which cannot be ignored.

It is still widely assumed in public discussion that in the interest of 'harmonious community relations' the minorities *ought* to assimilate themselves culturally. If such an argument is accepted, it follows that the provision of any kind of differential service should be opposed on the grounds that it will hinder the achievement of wider goals of public policy. However, much more consideration needs to be given as to whether assimilation is either a likely or a practicable means whereby the wider problems might be resolved. The underlying assumption of this paper is that it is not. On the contrary, members of the many minorities have organised, and are continuing to organise, their lives in a distinctive manner. While members of the older generation have simply drawn upon familiar values to build a comfortable and convenient world around themselves, members of the younger generation are utilising their ethnic resources both to resist pressures put upon them by the majority, and to challenge the unequal position in which they find themselves. Such processes are likely to continue for the forseeable future. As has been argued elsewhere (Ballard and Driver, 1979) assimilation is an unrealistic basis for public policy: what is urgently required is recognition of both the existence and the legitimacy of ethnic interests, whatever they may be.

All discussions in the field of race and ethnic relations necessarily have political overtones. For instance, one contemporary expression of majority interests is hostility towards non-European minorities. Such hostility arises partly because the minorities are perceived as competitors for scarce resources, and partly because it is becoming increasingly obvious that their members are sustaining their communal distinctiveness. Yet ethnic aggregations are maintained in quite large part precisely in reaction to external hostility. Many Britons of non-European origin are deeply suspicious of all members of the dominant majority. From a majority perspective there is a strong tendency to assume that cultural factors lie at the root of most minority problems (perhaps because such a view is the least disturbing), but it should not be forgotten that discrimination is one of the most overwhelming problems with which they have to deal. It seems probable that most professionals in the social services underestimate the extent and significance of racial inequality. Certainly most Asians and West Indians believe that they do.

Even when practitioners do recognise the existence of such inequalities, a whole series of problems and dilemmas still remains. To what extent should problems presented by individuals be related back solely to the question of racial inequality? Should members of the minorities be encouraged to ignore the inequity of the treatment they receive? Or should they be encouraged to challenge it? If so, how should they go about it? If young people are rejecting the values of both the majority and their parents (although for different reasons), what kind of styles are they likely to adopt? How can they best be helped to find appropriate and viable solutions? It is not yet possible even to begin to give answers to most of these questions, not least because a variety of solutions is still being explored.

Finally, although discussion of the practicalities of the provision of effective services for the ethnic minorities is almost inevitably shot through by political and ideological dilemmas, the issues raised can nevertheless be approached on a straightforward professional level. For the practitioner the question of whether the minorities ought, or ought not, to remain ethnically distinct should be irrelevant. The fact is that they *are*. In so far as his specialism, whatever it is, demands that he should take into account the social and cultural worlds in which his clients live, he needs to make a response to ethnic diversity. If he does not, his practice is inadequate in purely professional terms.

8

This last paper, while illustrating the need for the type of fundamental re-assessments suggested in Ballard (above), demonstrates what can be done with a flexible approach and a degree of determination even under present circumstances. The diagnostic difficulties of Western-trained psychiatrists faced with manifes-tations of stress and mental illness in a cross-cultural situation; the suggested reasons for South Asians' underutilisation of psychiatric services; the main causes of stress and illness exhibited by patients: all of these were recognised by the author and his fellow practitioners as indicators of their inability to provide an effective service to non-indigenous patients. Improvements were achieved by efforts to communicate with and understand the background of patients, and by the re-assessment of diagnostic categories and methods of treatment. These measures entailed a clinical team encompassing a variety of skills, and engaging in a dialogue with members of local minorities and academics and researchers in various fields.

Diagnosing Mental Illness

Asians and the psychiatric services[1]

Philip Rack

To leave home and go to live in another place is never a light undertaking, especially if the distance is great and the move a long-term one. Migration is inevitably accompanied by emotional stress. There is grief at parting. The journey may be full of new experiences, some exciting, others frightening and intense if life hitherto has been confined within local horizons. There may be helplessness induced by a strange language, the fear of misunderstanding or being misunderstood, changes of climate and diet, being physically distinctive, feeling unwelcome, experiencing social isolation and dependence on strangers. In addition to these common stresses, more specific anxieties affect particular groups. The refugee who leaves a homeland torn by violence may carry a burden of grief or uncertainty about the fates of family and friends, perhaps tinged with guilt. The displaced person may be exposed to the initiative-sapping institutionalisation of a transit camp. The migrant worker, forced by poverty to seek his fortune abroad, may have good reason to worry about the conditions in which he has left his family. The young man who sets out boldly for Eldorado may require instant success to justify his decision (and repay the debts he has incurred). A bride may be joining a husband she hardly knows, but on whom she will be utterly dependent.

After the initial shocks, other stresses may follow. The craftsman or skilled worker may be stripped of his status and reduced to the rank of labourer, highly prized skills counting for nothing in the new environment. Cultural norms may be rudely challenged. The habit patterns and value systems which were part of the individual's sense of identity may be undermined, so the migrant may find disquieting changes occurring within his own mental processes. At a later stage in the settlement process, parents may find their children growing away from them, adopting manners, modes and morals of the new culture, for which the parents are not prepared (see C. Ballard, this volume).

In view of these difficulties it would not be surprising to discover a high prevalence of psychiatric breakdown and other stress-related disorders among migrants. This has been demonstrated in several epidemiological studies in America (Pollock, 1913; Odegaard, 1932; Ruesch *et al.*, 1948; Malzberg, 1969); England (Hemsi, 1967; Hashmi, 1968); and Australia (Cade & Krupinski, 1962; Krupinski*et al.*, 1965a, 1965b; Krupinski, 1967; 1973). By contrast, a number of other studies indicate a low rate of illness among some groups of migrants (Odegaard, 1945; Murphy, 1959, 1965, 1973; Hitch, 1975; von Cranach, 1976; Cochrane, 1976). (The subject has been well reviewed by Murphy, 1976.)

To explore the subject further it is necessary to abandon generalisations and ask specific questions. For example: if Asian immigrants in Britain consult psychiatrists less often, and Polish immigrants more often, than the general population is this because one group is 'healthier' or 'better adjusted', or because they regard psychiatrists and medical services differently? If young West Indians in Brixton appear more frequently in courts than in clinics, is this because they signal their distress by anti-social acts rather than by symptoms? If Dutch migrants in Canada seem remarkably free of mental illness (Murphy, 1976) is this because of the process of selection? If paranoid symptoms seem to be common among Polish immigrants (Hitch and Rack, 1976) and depression under-represented among West Indians and Asians (Littlewood and Lipsedge, 1976), can we be sure of diagnostic accuracy, or could the doctors be misled by cultural differences?

Answers to questions of this kind cannot be given until psychiatry and related disciplines have built up a substantial volume of case lore on different groups. As a contribution to this process we offer some observations on psychiatric illness among Pakistanis in an English industrial city, as observed by a clinical team at Lynfield Mount Hospital, Bradford, during the period 1972–76. This hospital provides a fairly comprehensive psychiatric service to the urban centre of Bradford Metropolitan District, which has a population of about 300,000. The hospital opened in 1966 and by 1972 the basic psychiatric service was fairly well established, and the staff began to turn their attention to particular special needs. Among other things, the service provided for immigrants was felt to be inadequate. The population served includes approximately 30,000 first-generation immigrants from the Indian sub-continent, of whom the majority (about 25,000) come from Pakistan. Some demographic and socio-logical characteristics of this group have been described by Saifullah Khan (this volume and 1974, 1976a, 1976b, 1976c, 1977). A multi-disciplinary team of psychiatrists, nurses, a social worker, a psychologist and an occupational therapist came together from the existing hospital staff, to pay special attention to immigrants' prob-lems. The work of this team has been described elsewhere (Commun-ity Relations Commission, 1976; Rack, 1976).

In 1971 a local survey revealed that Asian immigrants accounted for only 4 per cent of all referrals to Lynfield Mount Hospital. Since the local population was approximately 10 per cent Asian, some explanation of the discrepancy was required.[2] Several factors may be suggested. First, the atypical age structure; those who came as fit young adults had not yet reached the age of maximum psychiatric morbidity. Second, self-selection of migrants may be thought to 'weed out the unfit' (this is debatable). Third, the stigma of insanity – Asians' attitudes to mental illness resemble those generally held in England thirty years ago. Fourth, a reluctance to seek outside help for any personal problems which could be settled within the family. Fifth, the alternative option of going home: if depressed or anxious it would be natural to attribute this to being in Britain. Sixth, the ineffective-ness of the treatment offered: of those who came many must have gone away feeling that their problem was not understood, and were unlikely to recommend the service to their friends. Even when some therapeutic success had been achieved, there were the problems of a strange hospital environment with unfamiliar customs, language and food.

Underutilisation of services by first-generation immigrants is not confined to psychiatry, but extends to most welfare provision. The findings of McCulloch and his associates (Smith and McCulloch, 1976) show that immigrants are even more ignorant than the in-digenous population about sources of official help, and there are also cultural differences as to what constitutes a 'medical' problem. Such differences bedevil – and perhaps invalidate – any estimates of pre-valence which are based on referral data. This is so for psychiatric morbidity in general. It is even more true for estimates of prevalence of particular syndromes.

The next sections describe some aspects of the clinical presentations of various psychiatric syndromes among Asians in Bradford,[3] and some of the psycho-social stresses which affect this population and may contribute to breakdowns. Observations are based on clinical experience not on research data. They are impressionistic and subject to continuous revision.

Some 300 Asian patients were referred to Lynfield Mount in the period 1972–76. To classify them into percentages of neurotics, schizophrenics, etc., is a difficult and unrewarding exercise; certainly there are a number of clearly identifiable cases of schizophrenia, manic-depressive psychosis and so on, but diagnostic categories are not very precise in psychiatry. In the diagnostic process of discriminating physical from mental illness, and within mental illness separating psychosis from neurosis, the psychiatrist is influenced by what the patient says and how he says it and by the *pattern* of symptoms presented. For example, palpitations, sweating, headache or insomnia will be recognised as more likely to be psychiatric (among British patients), whereas persistent hiccups or pain in the knee are more likely to be organic. Hallucinations are not usually neurotic but more often psychotic.[4] These are not reliable discriminators but they are pointers: diagnosis depends on recognising possibilities and following them up, and efficiency depends on following up the most likely ones first; so we need to consider cultural differences in symptoms to which the British doctor should be alert.

Depression

For example, take the case of an English woman of menopausal age who attends the clinic complaining of 'depression'. On enquiry she may be found to be weepy, hopeless for the future, full of guilt and self-denigration. If she has insomnia and early waking, loss of appetite and weight, loss of libido, constipation, various musculo-skeletal aches and pains, these all add together to build a picture suggesting the clinical entity known as *endogenous depression*.

Consider next a Pakistani woman of similar age. This patient complains of pain and weakness. On enquiry it may be learned that she also has insomnia, loss of appetite and weight, constipation, etc. and perhaps she may also admit to feeling depressed and hopeless. It is clearly the same syndrome, and will respond to the same treatment, but the manner of presentation is different. The English woman produces her emotional distress first, and her physical complaints as an afterthought, whereas the Pakistani woman produces physical symptoms and makes no reference to her mood. Indeed, she may not say that she is depressed even when asked directly about this. The psychiatrist is then in the position of having to diagnose 'endogenous depression' in the absence of the depressed mood which he customarily regards as its cardinal symptom.

Why would she not mention the disorder of mood? Leff has suggested that it may be partly a matter of language (1973). In Pushtu, for example, there is no word for 'depression', and one can only say, 'My heart is tired'. The English patient could equally well say, 'I am heartbroken', but this is understood as a metaphor. More explicit words are available in English but not in Pushtu. In another example from Nigeria, the same word in Yoruba suffices for both 'angry' and 'sad'. No discrimination is made between adverse emotional states which Europeans distinguish clearly. We may describe Pushtu and Yoruba as 'primitive' languages, and the same could be said for Punjabi and colloquial village Urdu (literary Urdu is another matter); but 'primitive' is a condescending term which may mislead. Surely the point is that in any language a rich vocabulary is developed in subjects which seem important to the people concerned. The Laplanders are reported to have many different words for snow, presumably because fresh snow, last year's snow, powdery snow, crisp snow, snow on which one can or cannot sledge all require to be differentiated. Contemporary English is remarkably rich in words to describe mood states. As well as 'depressed' one could be despondent, despairing, dispirited, disillusioned, disconsolate, gloomy, melancholy, miserable, morbid, morose, unhappy . . . or just sad. Quite a lot of these words are actually used in everyday speech, and not as *synonyms*, but with fine shades of meaning, as in – 'he is *sad* (about the death of his dog) but he isn't *miserable* about it'. The exchange, 'Are you *depressed*?' – 'No, but I am *unhappy*' – seems to mean something even if its meaning would be hard to pin down. In contrast to this rich vocabulary with which we describe internal experience, English is strangely deficient in some other ways. For example, *my brother-in-law* may be either *my wife's brother* or *my sister's husband* – two very different relationships. *Cousin* means many things, each of which merits a different word in some other languages. Differentiation between *gran* and *nan* (paternal grandmother and maternal grandmother) has all but died out. Can it be that we are intensely concerned (preoccupied, obsessed) with our own internal experiences (internal well-being, self-realisation, self-fulfilment, exploration of inner space), whereas some other cultures find this less interesting, and concentrate more on a person's relationships in society, his performance of social and functional roles? This suggestion does not imply that the Urdu-speaker is incapable of experiencing the whole range of emotion, or is insensitive to fine shades of feeling (the wealth of Indian classical art and poetry contradicts any such idea); but perhaps they are not very important subjects on which to focus day-to-day attention and thereby develop a colloquial vocabulary or use them as primary symptoms of disease. To explain all differences of symptom presentation in terms of linguistics is certainly an oversimplification, but this hypothesis serves as a reminder, if nothing more, of two features commonly observed in Asian patients, namely *somatisation* and *illness as social dysfunction*.

Somatisation

The tendency to focus on bodily complaints has been noted in several Asian and African psychiatric studies (for example Carstairs, 1975). It has certain pitfalls for the British doctor. If he is too much impressed by physical symptoms, this can lead to unnecessary X-rays, blood tests and referrals to specialists, which miss the point and reinforce the patient's belief in himself as physically sick.[5]

A second danger is that the doctor, having excluded physical disease, shrugs the symptoms off on the grounds that 'all Asians are hypochondriacs'. 'Hypochondriasis' is never a sufficient diagnosis. It has a variety of possible causes including depressive illness which will respond to the appropriate drug treatment, and anxiety neurosis for which some form of psychotherapy is appropriate.

As already noted, generalised weakness, in the sense of 'I have lost all my strength', and diffuse pains throughout the body and limbs (best described as 'body-ache'), are often the first complaints of Pakistani patients suffering from anxiety or depression. Impotence, both erectile and ejaculatory, are often mentioned by men, frequently accompanied by the conviction that they are leaking sperm in their urine (spermatorrhoea – the so-called *Dhat* syndrome). English men in states of anxiety or depression may well have some degree of impotence but they do not usually produce it as the first symptom mentioned, and never complain of spermatorrhoea. It has been suggested that the 'Asian Syndrome' of impotence, spermatorrhoea, backache, headache and generalised weakness, is related to the belief that seminal fluid is stored in the head and spinal cord. Pakistani women seldom complain spontaneously of frigidity (but it must be noted nor do many English women). They are particularly conscious of menstrual irregularities and attach great importance to them. Another complaint is 'something wrong with the bowels' – not constipation, nor diarrhoea, nor flatulence, nor pain, but 'something' which cannot be pinned down. Similarly 'something wrong with the eyes' – not pain, or blurred or restricted vision – just 'something wrong'.

An important part of the diagnostic process is the patient's manner at interview, and here there may be cultural differences. An English patient who delivers a long list of complaints in enthusiastic detail and with a smile on his face is already halfway to a diagnosis of hysteria. The same smile from an Asian may indicate shy politeness, and the detail reflects the 'somatic' preoccupation. Cultural differences in the extent of permitted emotional expression are well known, for example, Giel's observation that Ethiopian patients act in a manner which seems 'hysterical' (Giel, 1976) or the anonymous comment that all residents of the Orkney Islands seem to be depressed. In global terms the Englishman's stiff upper lip is a local peculiarity.

Illness as social dysfunction

Consider the following scene. The patient, a Pakistani woman, was discharged from hospital a month earlier after successful treatment of puerperal psychosis. She has returned to the clinic for a follow-up visit accompanied by her husband.

British psychiatrist How is your wife getting on now?
Husband Oh, she's very well now, doctor. She's fine. Thank you so much. She is looking after the house. She is doing the cooking, she is caring for the baby. I am working again now. She is cured. Thank you. . .
Psychiatrist Good, I am so glad she is able to do those things, but, tell me, how does she feel in herself?
(Brief conversation between husband and wife.)
Husband She's very well, doctor. She's looking after the family. She is doing the cooking . . .

Psychiatrist Yes, yes, but please ask her how she is feeling – does she *feel* well – does she feel *happy?*
(*A further lengthy conversation, husband and wife both evidently perplexed.*)
Husband   She is very happy now doctor because she is able to do the cooking, care for the baby, clean the house. Thank you very much . . .

This is not a verbatim account and the conversation has been abbreviated, but the experience is in essence a familiar one, and the message which seems to come across is that the important criterion of health is the ability to fulfil one's role, carry out one's obligations. Personal happiness, contentment, satisfaction, are doubtless very important; but internal distress is not illness, and distress as such is not discussed with doctors. Illness is indicated by the presence of other symptoms and its severity is judged by the degree of social dysfunction.

If this is a correct interpretation, some may feel that it is a viewpoint which makes good sense, and a useful corrective to the view increasingly prevalent in English society, that all distress is in some way 'pathological' and should be relieved by doctors. This view has probably arisen because there are some illnesses (for example, endogenous depression) in which to all intents and purposes the distress *is* the illness. In a culture in which that is not recognised, the psychiatrist would see fewer cases of depression, and only those with conspicuous social dysfunction.

Another consequence of the illness/social dysfunction equation is that illness is not a private affair, but a matter of public concern. Whereas an English family will usually assume that the doctor wishes to be alone with his patient, an Asian family are more likely to crowd into the consulting room together and share in the history-taking, violating the (English) doctor's culturally-determined ideas about patient privacy and confidentiality.

Schizophrenia

Clinical reports from many countries suggest that an illness recognisable as schizophrenia exists in most ethnic and cultural groups, but with local variants in symptom-pattern and considerable differences in incidence-estimates. These reports are supported by the recent surveys conducted by WHO (1974). Schizophrenia certainly occurs among immigrants in Bradford, and can be diagnosed with reasonable confidence where thought disorder and fragmentation are present (but these are particularly difficult to demonstrate if there is a language barrier).

Paranoia (the belief that one is a victim of persecution) can be misleading. Many immigrants have in fact suffered persecution, and racial prejudice does exist. Even if it did not, one might predict that uprooting, cultural deprivation, social isolation and misunderstanding might favour a cautious, suspicious attitude which could spill over into paranoid misinterpretation. In a previous study (Hitch and Rack, 1976) we have noted an increased incidence of paranoid symptoms among immigrants from Eastern Europe (supporting the earlier findings of Krupinski *et al.*, 1973), but this tendency seems, inexplicably, less noticeable among Asian immigrants. Giel's studies of Ethiopian students show that a great deal depends on how the questions are phrased (Giel, 1976).

Even specific paranoid delusions accompanied by hallucinations are not necessarily diagnostic of schizophrenia. To come under the influence of supernatural forces by bewitchment or demon possession is a fairly common manifestation of hysteria especially among girls and young women (*vide* the Witches of Salem). Belief in the evil eye and the use of charms are widespread in rural Pakistan. If you become ill, especially if the illness is unfamiliar and recovery is delayed, it is quite natural to seek an explanation in terms of *bad kismat* (fate) or *nasr* (evil eye or envy) and to look around for the source which may be human or supernatural. This is also a popular explanation for infertility.

Such superstitions are not confined to the uneducated. The intelligent, sophisticated and seemingly Westernised Asian patient may have such explanations at the back of his or her mind. He or she will probably not mention them to an English doctor but may refer to them obliquely, saying with apparent irrelevance, 'There is a member of my family who dislikes me'. Some patients who accept psychiatric treatment also consult local lay healers at the same time, and may be noticed on examination to be wearing charms (commonly a piece of thread tied around a limb or digit). It is arguable that in cases of neurosis or situational anxiety the lay healers who command faith may be just as effective as the trained psychiatrist.

For the British doctor or social worker, the important thing to remember is that ideas of persecution, whether generalised or specific, do not point in the direction of schizophrenia (as they would in an English patient) but are consequences of the fact of being ill and worried about it.

A syndrome which must be distinguished from schizophrenia is the *acute schizophreniform stress reaction*. An English person under unmanageable stress may respond with anxiety, depression, hysteria or other *neurotic* symptoms; but he is unlikely to develop delusions, hallucinations, confusion, thought disorder and other signs of schizophrenia. When this does happen in an English patient it is often interpreted as evidence of an underlying schizophrenic predisposition and the stress is regarded as only a trigger factor. Among Asians, Africans and West Indians, however, such reactions are not uncommon. The presentation is indistinguishable from schizophrenia but the consequences are different. Whereas acute schizophrenia requires treatment by Phenothiazine drugs which should be continued for a long time afterwards to avoid relapses, the *acute schizophreniform stress reaction* tends to recover in a few days with minimal drug treatment if something is done about the causes of stress; and the prognosis is correspondingly better than for schizophrenia.

Neuroses and other stress reactions

In the practice of psychiatric diagnosis the clinician seeks to recognise syndromes – symptom-clusters – which point in the direction of causes. Indications of physical disease must be followed up by appropriate investigations. If a psychosis is diagnosed, the search for causes is abandoned (or, rather, it is left to the research worker) but certain well-established lines of treatment are indicated. If neurosis or psychosomatic illness is diagnosed, however, the diagnosis is incomplete until the stresses and conflicts which are producing the maladaptive response have been elucidated. Since the patient is usually unaware of the connection between the symptoms and the stresses, he does not volunteer this information and it has to be sought. In Asian patients in particular, evidence of stress is often very difficult to obtain since the patient himself sees his illness in purely physical terms, and resists, even resents, questions about social and emotional conflicts. One is often left guessing about concealed anxieties, and the doctor (or nurse or social worker) most familiar with the social and cultural background is the most likely to guess correctly. No two people have the same problems, but a few generalisations may be offered.

Ambitions

For any individual, anxiety is engendered most in those areas of life in which success is most highly prized, and there are general cultural differences in emphasis. In village Pakistan, fertility is crucial. A barren woman is a failure, fit to be discarded. Impotence is a serious threat to a man's self-esteem, and thereby often perpetuated. If a couple have been married a year and the wife is not yet pregnant, this may well have a bearing on the symptoms. Material and financial success are highly valued, and for most migrants in Britain the motive for migration. Inevitably many migrants do not achieve their own or their family's expectations. Many a foreign student of moderate ability aspires to academic achievements which are beyond his reach.

Morality

For orthodox Muslims, contemporary Western society is a moral quicksand. Islam provides rules which are directive and prescriptive, as does orthodox Judaism or Catholicism, and its rules are intertwined into the mores and detailed behaviour patterns of Muslim society. In England not only are the religious rules less precise and detailed, but they are no longer intertwined in secular life. Thus the Pakistani comes from a situation in which the canons of behaviour are clear, specific and widely accepted, to one in which individuation, self-determination and the right 'to do your own thing' are highly prized and there are few imposed sanctions. This is a threatening situation to which he may over-react in several different ways.

Family structure

Any immigrant who is joined in England by members of his extended family automatically accepts loyalty and responsibility for them, and often the traditional 'joint family system' is re-established in modified form. This system which works well enough in an unchanging rural setting comes under strain in any urban environment (Saifullah Khan, this volume). For example the authority of elders is most visibly exercised in relation to marriages and it is here that many problems arise.

A young man who comes to England unmarried, in his late teens (as many have done), will expect to make a return visit after a few years, for a marriage arranged by his family. If the young man was in England at a younger age and spent a significant time in English schools, when the call comes for him to return and be married he may rebel. Perhaps he is already friendly with a girl in England, or perhaps he wishes to make his own choice at a later stage. If he makes the trip home, he may reject the girl chosen in his absence, and feel justified in doing so. To a boy who was born in England the idea of going to Pakistan for an arranged marriage may be wholly repugnant: but even if his parents have been settled here for some years and have some sympathy with his views, they will find it difficult to support him against the grandparental pressures exerted from home. Such matters cannot be settled by correspondence, and a great deal of coming and going is usually involved before a compromise is reached, if indeed this is possible at all. The psychiatric out-patient clinic contains a number of young men who are contemplating a return trip to get married, and their conflicts frequently appear in the form of sexual anxieties.

For a young married couple living in England, the domestic situation differs from the traditional culture in ways which are not always anticipated. For example the marriage selection process may not be so efficient or scrupulous. Whereas traditionally the two families take care to achieve reasonable compatibility, negotiations in England may be entrusted to an intermediary who is not familiar with both parties. He could be influenced by other considerations, including the fact that there are many in Pakistan who wish to come to Britain and can achieve this through marriage to someone established here.

To the bride entering a traditional joint family her relationship with her mother-in-law is probably more crucial than her relationship with her husband. With up to a dozen people living in one household, personal tensions which arise are to some extent diluted by the size of the group and by conventions and role-acceptances built into the social structure. If a girl is so unfortunate as to find herself cast in the role of Cinderella she may pass a message to her own parents, who placed her in this situation, and they should take up the cudgels on her behalf. No family would wish it to be known that they were maltreating a daughter-in-law. There are some unfortunate Pakistani girls in England, whose marriages are unhappy, who are completely at the mercy of their husbands because they have no other relatives they can contact in this country.

Another important difference is that the girl may not be coming to take up residence in the home of her mother-in-law, but to live with her husband alone, which is a situation for which she has received no preparation. Even where there is mutual affection and kindness the intensity of emotional interdependence in a nuclear family situation may be difficult to cope with if one has grown up with the more 'diluted' group situation.

Inter-generation conflicts

A girl in a Pakistani village has few options. She is not expected to make any decision or show any initiative. The same girl, brought to England at an early age, attends school and develops personal ambitions. The ethos of the English educational system is that children should learn to think for themselves and form their own opinions. Although this ideal is much diluted in practice, teachers still look with favour on the 'bright child' who works things out for herself and challenges the conventional wisdom. But to be a 'bright child' in this sense is almost diametrically opposed to being a 'good child' in the eyes of Pakistani parents. While she has been developing, her parents may have learned little or no English and have had little contact with English society. The accounts given by Saifullah Khan and C. Ballard in this volume exemplify some of the conflicts which arise and which may have tragic consequences.

Such girls turn up from time to time on the doorsteps of social service agencies, police stations or at hospitals. Sometimes they come to the psychiatrist after taking overdoses. Admission to a psychiatric unit makes matters worse because now the girl is not only stigmatised 'bad' but is also by definition 'mad'. What is needed is an experienced case worker who understands the cultural conflict and can speak to the parents in their own language to try to bring about some reconciliation or compromise solution. Even if such a person can be found, the task is tremendous and usually fruitless. The parents will often make any promise to get the girl back indoors and avoid a public scandal. For the English would-be helper involved in such a situation the moral dilemma of aiding the girl's rebellion is intensified by the knowledge that a brown-skinned girl who cuts herself off from her own community is not by any means assured of a welcome in white society and is extremely vulnerable to exploitation which she is ill-equipped to resist. It must be realised, however, that the parental alternative may be simply to get the girl married as fast as possible, before she 'causes any further trouble'.

The conflicts which teenage boys have with their parents seem less drastic because boys are traditionally permitted more freedom, but some of them get caught up in the prevailing confusion about sexuality and permissiveness. An Asian boy who listens to his English friends and workmates boasting about their sexual adventures may make the mistake of believing them, and assume that indiscriminate promiscuity is an English cultural norm. If he acts on this assumption he is likely to be disappointed. If English girls reject his advances he may attribute this to colour prejudice. Not many Indian and Pakistani girls are permitted to mix freely with boys (but some of those who do escape chaperonage are more vulnerable because of their innocently romantic ideas). Since sexual prowess is an issue of great importance, it is not surprising that many young men in this situation develop anxiety symptoms and worry about their supposed unattractiveness or impotence especially when contemplating marriage. Sexual dysfunction is best treated in the setting of stable and permanent relationship, and it is difficult to give categorical reassurance about impotence to a man who is unmarried and has not yet seen his prospective bride. We have found, however, that in many cases the anxiety is based on ignorance of normal sexual function and can be relieved by simple explanations and sex education given in the clinic.

Conclusion

Cultural factors affect mental illness in many ways. The *psychoses* occur in all cultures, but there are differences in the symptoms which they produce. *Neuroses* and other *stress reactions* also vary, and correct diagnosis depends on an understanding of the psycho-social stresses to which the individual is exposed.

Most industrial centres in the developed world are to some extent multi-cultural and it is essential that psychiatrists and other health workers should recognise this cultural diversity and its clinical consequences. The Asian population of Bradford provides an example of this. There are probably just as many important differences in the mental health problems of other minority groups in other places.

Notes and References

Introduction

1. References to further reading have not been inserted throughout this introduction. Each chapter contains references relating to the specific subject of enquiry. Only a few general references are suggested here: Allen (1971); Hiro (1971); Krausz (1972); Lawrence (1974); Political and Economic Planning (1977); Rose (1969); Watson (1977). For a comprehensive bibliography on ethnic minorities in Britain (including such topics as health, education, social services, immigration etc) see The Runnymede Trust, *Briefing Paper* 6/77 (Nov 1977).

Chapter 1

1. The present paper is drawn largely from Chapters 2 and 4 of my D. Phil. thesis (Oakley, 1971).

2. For a note on official estimates of numbers involved and entry conditions, see Runnymede Trust (1975).

3. I am currently preparing for publication a more up-to-date outline of Cypriot settlement in Britain, drawing particularly on 1971 census materials.

4. For further information on Turkish Cypriots, see S. Ladbury, 'Turkish Cypriots: Ethnic Relations in London and Cyprus', in Watson (1977).

5. For a brief outline of the social organisation of Cypriot settlement in Britain, see Oakley (1970); George and Millerson (1967); P. M. Constantinides in Watson (1977).

6. For a fuller outline of the Cypriot social and cultural background see R. Oakley, 'The Cypriot Background', in Oakley (1968) and Loizos (1975).

7. Republic of Cyprus, Ministry of Finance, *Demographic Report* (Nicosia, annual; previously entitled *Vital and Migration Statistics*). On the official Cyprus migration statistics and problems of their interpretation, see Oakley (1971).

8. The official Cyprus migration statistics do not record the marital status of migrants, nor any other details of family composition. Marital status must be inferred from other data or derived from other sources. For women migrants, the most reliable indicator seems to be the figure of 62 per cent for those reporting their 'previous occupation' as 'housewife' (as a percentage of all female migrants no longer in full-time education) during the period 1960 to 1966. A survey of migrants arriving in 1958 found that 53 per cent of adult women were already married, but this lower figure covers only a single year, whereas the former covers a longer period including the peak years of the migration. See Nearchou (1960). For men, the only available indicator of marital composition is from a national sample survey of immigrants conducted in 1960, which found that of 61 per cent of respondents who were married, 60 per cent had been married in Cyprus. Allowing for the likelihood that some of these respondents had arrived in Britain as children, it may be estimated on the basis of this survey that around 45 per cent of Cypriot men have been married at the time of their departure.

9. This cannot be precisely measured from the migration statistics, although the general pattern can be inferred without difficulty. For example, mean family size among migrants is indicated by the fact that for every 'housewife' departing the island in 1960–66, the average number of children under fifteen was 1.3; the same figure is produced by taking the average number of children per adult woman among those admitted to Britain as 'dependants' during the period mid-1960 to 1966.

10. Main findings published by the Economist Intelligence Unit, *Commonwealth Immigrants in Britain* (London, 1961); these unpublished data made available by Mass Observation.

11. Information on visiting is derived from *Vital and Migration Statistics/Demographic Reports*.

12. On the character and significance of 'friendship' as contrasted with kinship, see Loizos (1975); in this case, kinship is clearly subordinate. Friendship allows non-kin (or other than close kin) to establish a contractual bond on the basis of equality, as opposed to the inequality inherent in patronage.

13. On 'patronage' in Cyprus, see Loizos (1975), and in the Mediterranean area generally, see Davis (1976) and Gellner and Waterbury (1977).

14. On 'spiritual kinship' in Cyprus, see Loizos (1975).

15. Information concerning the work of the Welfare Department is drawn from Republic of Cyprus, *Reports of the Department of Social Services* (Nicosia, annual reports); and from interviews conducted with officers of the Department in 1965.

16. *Report of the Department of Social Welfare Services* (1963).

17. In 1957 and 1958, 24 and 15 children respectively were reunited with their parents; in 1965 and 1966, the only other years for which figures are available, the numbers were 8 and 5 children respectively.

18. In 1965 and 1966 it handled 153 and 118 cases respectively.

19. There were three categories of vouchers, A, B and C: Category A for those with a specific job to come to, Category B for those possessing certain skills or qualifications, and a residual Category C for those applicants not qualifying for the preceding two. Priority was given to Categories A and B,

while Category C vouchers were issued on a 'first come-first served basis'. But within just over two years, despite a massive waiting list, Category C vouchers were no longer being issued due to a severe cut-back in overall numbers admitted; moreover, for Category A, there was by the end of 1966 a waiting list of at least a year.

Chapter 2

1. This paper is based on research carried out in 1971 to 1973 in Bradford and in Mirpur. The research involved living with a Mirpuri family in both settings (that is, in Mirpur with the parents and siblings of the wife in the Bradford household), participating in their daily life and establishing a (their) network of contacts with many other families who were friends and relatives. The most detailed findings are available in Saifullah Khan (1974) and a résumé of this doctoral thesis can be found in Saifullah Khan (1977).

2. There is little detailed material of village life in northern Pakistan. Suggested reading includes Ahmad (1977), Alavi (1972) and Eglar (1960).

3. Many Indian women, although coping with the double jobs of home and work have the advantage of a busy daily routine, company at work and, in the long run, greater access to and understanding of the outside world. Although many Indian women work or interact mostly with their countrywomen they are more likely to acquire a certain linguistic and social confidence as well as an appreciation of the influence of the wider society on their children. See Saifullah Khan (1979).

4. This paper has restricted discussion to the first-generation Mirpuris who have migrated to Britain. For discussion of some likely trends in the second generation see C. Ballard, this volume.

Chapter 3

1. Joint roles involve husband and wife carrying out activities together, or the same activity being carried out by either partner at different times. A segregated marital role relationship is one in which complementary and independent types of organisation predominate. There is a clearly defined division of labour into male tasks and female tasks and the couple expect to have different leisure pursuits. (These definitions are based on Bott, 1957.)

2. The fieldwork on which this paper is based was carried out between 1970 and 1972 in London. The first phase involved a survey of 300 families living in four inner-London boroughs: Brent, Hammersmith, Lambeth and Hackney. In the second phase Miss Muir visited twenty families several times over a period of eighteen months, making detailed notes on each visit, and also getting certain systematic information from each family. The twenty families

in the second phase of the study were selected either with the help of the Commonwealth Students' Children's Society (whose most generous assistance we gratefully acknowledge) or through introductions by mutual acquaintances. Because of the need to match characteristics in these twenty families a random sample was not practicable. It is the intensive second phase of the study which provided the data for the present paper. All names are of course fictitious and we have also changed certain other details to assure anonymity to the families who helped us.

3. Bott uses the term conjugal relations and it is normally employed by the authors of this paper. However, for the purposes of this volume 'conjugal' has been replaced by 'marital' throughout and the term 'tension' has been replaced by 'stress'.

4. The degree or measure of role stress was assessed from the extensive notes kept on visits made to each family over several months. At the analysis stage, these notes were coded for references to each of the activity areas – chores, finances, decisions, leisure, parental role and communication, and then scored from 0 to 10 for indications of stress in each activity area.

5. See note 3 above.

6. The detailed numerical indices are presented and analysed in Goody and Muir (1973). The discussion presented here is based on this detailed analysis.

7. The rating of marital role stress consisted of ratings on stress over dominance, extra-marital affairs, wife's job, and the expression of opinions in politics, etc. It will be seen that although these items are related to those used for rating jointness of marital role they are in fact not the same.

8. For the decision-making sphere, stress scores were originally divided into high, moderate and low, rather than dichotomised into high and low as for the other activity spheres. For the summary table the eight 'moderate' stress scores have been divided between 'high' and 'low' categories.

9. Since we originally selected our intensive sample so that an equal number of Ibo and Ashanti couples had fostered children in England, this material cannot be used to study the relative preferences between ethnic groups for fostering. The low number of Ibo and Ashanti among West Africans in the survey makes it difficult to use this as a basis for comparing the incidence of fostering between the two groups.

10. See Forde and Jones (1950); Green (1947); Isichei (1976); Meek (1937); and Uchendu (1965) for accounts of Ibo traditional society.

11. See Fortes (1949, 1950, 1969) and Rattray (1923) for accounts of Ashanti traditional society.

Chapter 4

1. The material reported in this paper is drawn from a research programme within the SSRC Research Unit on Ethnic Relations at the University of Bristol. The research was led by P. Weinreich and the other members of the

team were A.K. Brah, M.I. Fuller, D. Loudon and R. Miles. The original design of the research derived from a conceptual scheme elaborated in P. Weinreich's doctoral dissertation; the methodology was later developed in collaboration. The computer program used in this research to calculate indices of identity structure was devised by P. Weinreich with the assistance of I. Carr and A. French.

2. The definition of a person's identification conflict with another is a multiplicative function of his current- and contra-identifications with that other. As current- and contra-identifications with the other simultaneously increase so will his conflict in identification become greater.

3. The Asian category included adolescents from a variety of ethnic and religious backgrounds (including Muslim Punjabi Pakistanis, Sikh and Hindu Punjabi Indians, and a Christian Pakistani). The majority of the West Indian category were Jamaicans.

4. Much of the American research forms (as a result of particular methods used and the prevailing interpretations of the data) the consensus that black people were fundamentally damaged. They were seen as the victims of discrimination and as devaluing their own people in line with the majority society's view of them. As a consequence, the consensus ran, their self-concepts were synonymous with self-hatred, self-rejection, and the 'mark of oppression' (on children: Clark and Clark, 1947; Goodman, 1946; Horowitz, 1939; Lasker, 1929; Minard, 1931; Morland, 1963, 1966; Trager and Yarrow, 1952; on psychiatric patients: Grier and Cobbs, 1968; Kardiner and Ovessey, 1951; the consensus is repeated in: Banks, 1972; Isaacs, 1975; Poussaint and Atkinson, 1972; Stein, 1975: for a critical review that challenges the consensus: Thomas and Sillin, 1972). These commentators could not see any signs of relief from this gloomy picture. There were no predictions in these studies about changes in identity towards black consciousness and 'black is beautiful'. Although other studies with children have indicated different results which have been put down either to *effects* of changes in the social climate (Black is Beautiful, Hraba and Grant, 1970), or to artefacts of the methods used (Greenwald and Oppenheim, 1968), the point remains that the consensus became widespread and, more importantly, there were no predictions of *subsequent* changes.

Chapter 5

1. The term South Asian refers to (the children of) Indian, Pakistani, Bangla Deshi and East African Asians. This paper was prepared for a non-specialist audience and the author's aim was to highlight the main and common features experienced by adolescents of this general category.

2. The fieldwork was carried out in conjunction with Roger Ballard, see R. Ballard this volume.

3. Suggested reading on South Asians in Britain include: Community Relations Commission (1976); Crishna (1975); James (1974); Taylor (1976); Thompson (1974); Vatuk (1972).

4. While there will continue to be many differences between and within the various (Asian) ethnic categories (due to cultural, socio-economic and personality factors, etc.) it is likely that the more specific ethnic and religious boundaries will decrease among the second and third generations. However, an increasing number of adolescents may perceive of themselves as belonging to a wider 'Asian' or 'British Asian' category and this will not necessarily involve (as is often assumed) a decrease in distinctive identity and values. For another example of emerging 'Asian ethnicity' see Saifullah Khan (1979).

Chapter 6

1. The research was undertaken in 1971 to 1973. During this period I was engaged in observing and reporting upon the curricular, extra-curricular and leisure activities of Form IV pupils, and in interviewing pupils, teachers, parents, administrators and others directly or indirectly engaged in the school experiences of pupils in Form IV. Alongside the ethnographic information, statistical data was accumulated on the various tests and examination undergone by Form IV pupils from the eleven-plus examination to the CSE examinations at the end of their secondary school career.

2. For surveys of literature on these efforts, see Goldman and Taylor (1966), McNeal and Rogers (1971), Power (1967) and Schools Council (1967).

3. See Driver (1977).

Chapter 7

1. This research was carried out from 1971 to 1975 and there remains ongoing involvement to a less intensive degree. The researchers mentioned are myself and Catherine Ballard, whose contribution to this volume is also based on our joint field research.

2. Both these difficulties have been experienced by many of the contributors to this volume. The question of confidentiality is mentioned in the Preface. Objective commentary becomes increasingly difficult the more an observer is involved in the processes which he seeks to analyse. Although anthropologists expect to be participants as well as observers, those working in their own societies can anticipate much more active involvement. The experience brings its own rewards, but poses major problems at the levels of both ethics and analysis.

Chapter 8

1. Based on a lecture delivered to the Leeds Regional Psychiatric Association in February 1976 and reproduced by permission of the Association.

2. A high percentage of the South Asians in Bradford are Pakistanis (see Saifullah Khan in this volume). This survey and subsequent referral figures include other South Asian categories, for example Gujeratis, Sikhs and East African Asians.

3. It must be emphasised that statements such as 'Pakistani patients are . . . whereas English patients are . . .' should be read as a kind of short-hand. The similarities between these groups or any other groups of human beings far outweigh their differences, but it is the differences with which we are concerned here. The differences between individuals within either group far outweigh the differences between the groups, but in order to explore cultural differences at all, generalisations about groups have to be offered. Seen in a certain light any such generalisations may appear racist but this is certainly not intended.

4. These terms are used here in the sense currently accepted by most British psychiatrists. *Neurosis* implies a reaction to stress which is maladaptive in that the reaction does not help to resolve the stressful situation and may indeed aggravate it. *Anxiety states, phobic states, reactive depression* and *hysterical reactions* come under this heading. On the other hand *schizophrenia, endogenous depression* and *mania* are examples of psychosis, and are often attributed to disorders of brain chemistry though this is not proved. Stressful situations are not in themselves a sufficient cause of psychosis. Predisposed subjects may develop a psychosis without apparent stress, but stress may sometimes be implicated as a 'trigger factor'. It would be inappropriate to include here clinical descriptions of these various syndromes but the distinction between *neurosis* and *psychosis* is accepted as useful by nearly all practising British psychiatrists.

5. Physical illnesses must of course be excluded, and there are a few in particular which are easily overlooked. Osteomalacia due to Vitamin D deficiency (rare among the English but not so rare in Asian immigrant women and girls) can cause vague, diffuse, 'unconvincing' pains in the limbs. Weakness and general malaise may well be symptoms of depression or anxiety, but might be the symptoms of tuberculosis, intestinal worms or anaemia, all of which are commoner among Asian than among English patients.

Bibliography

AHMAD, S. (1977) *Class and Power in a Punjabi Village* (New York: Monthly Review Press).

AKRAM, M. (1974) *Where Do You Keep Your String Beds?* (London: Runnymede Trust).

——(1977) *Appeal Dismissed: The Final Report of the Investigation into Immigration Control Procedure in the Indian Sub-continent* (London: Runnymede Trust).

ALAVI, H. (1972) 'Kinship in West Punjab Villages', *Contributions to Indian Sociology*, New Series 6.

ALLEN, S. (1971) *New Minorities, Old Conflicts, Asian and West Indian Migrants in Britain* (New York: Random House).

BALLARD, R., and BALLARD, C. (1977) 'The Sikhs: The Development of South Asian Settlements in Britain', in J. L. Watson (ed.), *Between Two Cultures: Migrants and Minorities in Britain* (Oxford: Blackwell).

BALLARD, R., and DRIVER, G. (1979) 'The Ethnic Approach', in P. Worsley (ed.), *Social Problems in Modern Britain* (Harmondsworth: Penguin).

BANKS, J. A. (1972) 'Racial Prejudice and the Black Self-Concept', in J. A. Banks and J. D. Grambs (eds), *Black Self-Concept* (Maidenhead: McGraw-Hill).

BANNISTER, D., and FRANSELLA, F. (1972) *Inquiring Man: The Theory of Personal Constructs* (Harmondsworth: Penguin).

BANNISTER, D., and MAIR, J. M. M. (1968) *The Evaluation of Personal Constructs* (London: Academic Press).

BIRMINGHAM COMMUNITY DEVELOPMENT PROJECT (1977) *People in Paper Chains, Final Report*, No. 3, Immigration and the State (Social Evaluation Unit, Oxford University).

BOTT, E. (1957) *Family and Social Network* (London: Tavistock).

CADE, J. F. J., and KRUPINSKI, J. (1962) 'Incidence of Psychiatric Disorders in Victoria in Relation to Country of Birth', *Medical Journal of Australia* 1:400.

CARSTAIRS, G. M. (1975) 'Measuring Psychiatric Morbidity in a South Indian Population', *Bulletin of British Psychology Society*.

CHEETHAM, J. (1972) *Social Work with Immigrants* (London: Routledge and Kegan Paul).

CLARK, B. R. (1962) *Educating the Expert Society* (San Francisco: Chandler).

CLARK, K. B., and CLARK, M. P. (1947) 'Racial Identification and Preference in Negro Children', in T. M. Newcomb and E. L. Hartley (eds), *Readings in Social Psychology* (New York: Henry Holt).

COCHRANE, R. (1976) 'Immigration and Mental Hospital Admissions: A Study of Rates for England and Wales 1971', *Social Psychiatry* (in press).

COMMUNITY RELATIONS COMMISSION (1976) *Aspects of Mental Health in a Multicultural Society*, C. Carmichael and J. Schlicht (eds) (London: Community Relations Council).

——(1976) *Between Two Cultures: A Study of Relationships in the Asian Community in Britain* (London: Community Relations Council).

——(1977) *Urban Deprivation, Racial Inequality and Social Policy: A Report* (London: HMSO).

VON CRANACH, M. (1976) 'Psychiatric Disorders among Foreign Workers in the Federal Republic of Germany', Presented at Symposium über Fragen der Transkulturell – vergleichen Psychiatrie in Europa, Kiel, April 1976.

CRISHNA, S. (1975) *Girls of Asian Origin in Britain* (London: YWCA).

CRISSMAN, L. W. (1975) 'The Individual Nature of Culture', unpublished paper prepared for the Central States Anthropological Association Meeting.

DAHYA, BADR. (1973) 'Pakistanis in Britain. Transients or Settlers', *Race*, 14.

——(1974) 'The Nature of Pakistanti Ethnicity in Industrial Cities in Britain', in A. Cohen (ed.), *Urban Ethnicity* (London: Tavistock).

DAVIS, J. (1976) *The People of the Mediterranean* (London: Routledge and Kegan Paul).

DRIVER, G. (1977) 'Ethnicity, Cultural Competence and School Achievement: A Case-study of West Indian Pupils attending a British Secondary Modern School', unpublished doctoral dissertation (Illinois: University of Illinois).

EGLAR, Z. (1960) *A Punjabi Village in Pakistan* (New York: Columbia University Press).

ERIKSON, E. H. (1959) 'The Problem of Ego Identity', *Psychological Issues*, 1.

——(1968) *Identity, Youth and Crisis* (New York: Norton).

FITZHERBERT, K. (1967) *West Indian Children in London* (London: Bell).

FOOT, P. (1965) *Immigration and Race in British Politics* (Harmondsworth: Penguin).

FORDE, D., and JONES, G. I. (1950) *The Ibo and Ibibio-speaking Peoples of South-eastern Nigeria* (London: International African Institute).

FORTES, M. (1949) 'Time and Social Structure: an Ashanti Case Study' in M. Fortes (ed.), *Social Structure* (London. Reprinted 1970, Athlone Press. London School of Economics).

——(1950) 'Kinship and Marriage among the Ashanti', in A. R. Radcliffe-Brown, and D. Forde (eds), *African Systems of Kinship and Marriage* (London: Oxford University Press).

—— (1969) *Kinship and the Social Order* (Chicago: Aldine Publishing Company).

GELLNER, E., and WATERBURY, J. (1977) *Patrons and Clients in Mediterranean Studies* (London: Duckworth).

GEORGE, V. and MILLERSON, G. (1967) 'The Cypriot Community of London', *Race*, VII, January.

GIEL, R. (1976) 'Problems of Transcultural Communication', Presented at International Congress of Transcultural Psychiatry, Bradford.

GOLDMAN, R. and TAYLOR, F. H. (1966) 'Coloured Immigrant Children: A Survey of Recent Studies and Literature on their Educational Problems and Potential', *Educational Research*, 8.

GOODENOUGH, W. (1971) *Culture, Language and Society* (Reading, Massachusetts: Addison, Wesley).

GOODMAN, M. E. (1946) 'Evidence Concerning the Genesis of Interracial Attitudes', *American Anthropologist*, 48.

GOODY, E. N., and MUIR, C. (1973) *Factors Relating to the Delegation of Parental Roles among West Africans in London* (London: SSRC).

—— (1977) 'The Quest for Education: West Africans in London', in J. L. Watson (ed.), *Between Two Cultures: Migrants and Minorities in Britain* (Oxford: Blackwell).

GREEN, M. M. (1947) *Ibo Village Affairs* (London: Sidgwick and Jackson).

GREENWALD, H. J., and OPPENHEIM, D. B. (1968) 'Reported Magnitude of Self-misidentification among Negro Children – Artefact?', *Journal of Personality and Social Psychology*, 8.

GRIER, W. H., and COBBS, P. M. (1968) *Black Rage* (New York Basic Books).

HASHMI, F. (1968) 'Community Psychiatric Problems among Birmingham Immigrants', *Journal of Social Psychiatry*, 2.

HAUSER, S. T. (1971) *Black and White Identity Formation* (New York: Wiley).

HEMSI, L. K. (1967) 'Psychiatric Morbidity of West Indian Immigrants', *Social Psychiatry*, 2.

HIRO, D. (1971) *Black British White British* (Harmondsworth: Penguin, in association with Eyre and Spottiswoode).

HITCH, P. J. (1975) 'Migration and Mental Illness in a Northern City', unpublished Ph.D. thesis (University of Bradford).

HITCH, P. J., and RACK, P. H. (1976) 'Paranoid Symptomatology among Polish Refugees in Britain', presented at Sumposim über Fragen der Transkulturell – Vergleichen Psychiatrie in Europa, Kiel, April 1976.

HOROWITZ, R. E. (1939) 'Racial Aspects of Self-Identification in Nursery School Children', *Journal of Psychology*, 7–8.

HRABA, J., and GRANT, G. (1970) 'Black is Beautiful: A Re-examination of Racial Preference and Identification', *Journal of Personality and Social Psychology*, 16.

HUNT, S. (1976) 'The Food Habits of Asian Immigrants' in *Getting the Most out of Food*, no. 11 (Burgess Hill: Van-den-Bergh and Jurgens).

—— (1977) 'Adaptation and Nutritional Implications of Food Habits among Uganda Asians Settling in Britain', unpublished Ph.D. thesis (London University).

ILLICH, I. (1975) *Medical Nemesis* (Harmondsworth: Penguin).

ISAACS, H. R. (1975) 'Basic Group Identity', in N. Glazer and D. P. Moynihan (eds), *Ethnicity* (Harvard University Press).

ISICHEI, E. (1976) *A History of the Igbo People* (London: Macmillan Press).

JAMES, A. G. (1974) *Sikh Children in Britain* (Oxford University Press for Institute of Race Relations).

JEFFERY, P. (1976) *Migrants and Refugees, Muslim and Christian Pakistani Families in Bristol* (Cambridge University Press).

JONES, C. (1976) *Immigration and Social Policy in Britain* (London: Tavistock).

KARDINER, A., and OVESSEY, L. (1951) *The Mark of Oppression* (New York: Norton).

KELLY, G. A. (1955) *The Psychology of Personal Constructs* (New York: Norton).

KRAUSZ, E. (1972) *Ethnic Minorities in Britain* (London: Paladin).

KRUPINSKI, J. (1967) 'Sociological Aspects of Mental Ill-health in Migrants', *Social Science and Medicine*, 1:267.

—— (1973) 'Psychological Maladaptation in Ethnic Concentrations in Victoria, Australia', Paper read at WFMH Congress, Sydney, October.

KRUPINSKI, J., SCHAECHTER, F., and CADE, J. F. J. (1965b) 'Factors Influencing the Incidence of Mental Disorders among Migrants', *Medical Journal of Australia*, 2:269.

KRUPINSKI, J., and STOLLER, A. (1965a) 'Incidence of Mental Disorders in Victoria According to Country of Birth', *Medical Journal of Australia*, 2:265.

KRUPINSKI, J., STOLLER, A., and WALLACE, L. (1973) 'Psychiatric Disorders in Eastern European Refugees now in Australia', *Social Science and Medicine*, 7:31.

LASKER, B. (1929) *Race Attitudes in Children* (New York: Henry Holt).

LAWRENCE, D. (1974) *Black Migrants White Natives. A Study of Race Relations in Nottingham* (Cambridge University Press).

LEFF, J. P. (1973) 'Culture and the Differentiation of Emotional States', *British Journal Psychiatry*, 123.

LITTLEWOOD, R., and LIPSEDGE, M. (1976) 'Migration, Ethnicity and Diagnosis'. Presented at International Congress Transcultural Psychiatry, Bradford, July.

LOIZOS, P. (1975) *The Greek Gift: Politics in a Cypriot Village* (Oxford: Blackwell).

McNEAL, J., and ROGERS, M. (1971) *The Multiracial School* (Harmondsworth: Penguin).

MALZBERG, B. (1969) 'Are Immigrants Psychologically Disturbed?', in S. C. Plog and R. E. Edgerton (eds), *Changing Perspectives in Mental Illness* (New York: Holt, Rinehart and Winston).

MEEK, C. K. (1937) *Law and Authority in a Nigerian Tribe* (London: Oxford University Press).

MINARD, R. D. (1931) 'Race Attitudes of Iowa Children', *Studies in Character*, vol. 4, no. 2. (University of Iowa).

MORLAND, J. K. (1963) 'Racial Self-Identification: A Study of Nursery School Children', *The American Catholic Sociological Review*, 24.

MORLAND, J. K. (1966) 'A Comparison of Race Awareness in Northern and Southern Children', *American Journal of Orthopsychiatry*, 36.

MUIR C., and GOODY, E. N. (1972) 'Student Parents: West African Families in London', *Race*, XIII, 3.

MURPHY, H. B. M. (1959) 'Culture and Mental Disorder in Singapore', in M. K. Opler (ed.), *Culture and Mental Health* (New York: Macmillan).

—— (1965) 'Migration and the Major Mental Disorders', in M. B. Kantor (ed.), *Mobility and Mental Health* (Springfield: Charles C. Thomas).

—— (1973) 'The Low Rate of Mental Hospitalisation shown by Immigrants to Canada', in C. A. Zwigmann and M. Pfeiffer-Ammade (eds), *Uprooting and After* (New York: Springer-Verlag).

—— (1976) 'Migration, Culture and Mental Health', paper presented at International Congress on Transcultural Psychiatry, Bradford, July.

NEARCHOU, V. (1960) 'The Assimilation of Cypriot Immigrants in London', MA thesis (University of Nottingham).

OAKLEY, R. (1968) *New Backgrounds: The Immigrant Child at Home and at School* (Oxford University Press for the Institute of Race Relations).

—— (1970) 'Cypriots in Britain', *Race Today*, April.

—— (1971) 'Cypriot Migration and Settlement in Britain', D. Phil (University of Oxford).

ODEGAARD, O. (1932) 'Emigration and Insanity', Supplement No. 4 to *Acta Psychiatrica Neurologica Scandinavica*, Copenhagen.

—— (1945) 'Distribution of Mental Diseases in Norway', *Acta Psychiatrica Neurologica Scandinavica*, 20.

OPPONG, C. (1974) *Marriage Among a Matrilineal Elite* (Cambridge University Press).

PARKER, S., and KLEINER, R. J. (1966) *Mental Illness in the Urban Negro Community* (New York: Free Press).

POUSSAINT, and ATKINSON, C. (1972) 'Black Youth and Motivation', in J. A. Banks and J. D. Grambs (eds), *Black Self-Concept* (Maidenhead: McGraw-Hill).

POLITICAL and ECONOMIC PLANNING (1977) *Racial Disadvantage in Britain*. Summary of PEP reports by David J. Smith (Harmondsworth: Penguin).

POLLOCK, H. M. (1913) 'A Statistical Study of the Foreign-born Insane in New York State Hospitals', *State Hospital Bulletin*, 19, 3, 5. 10–27 of special number.

POWER, J. (1967) *Immigrants in School: A Survey of Administrative Policies* (London: Council of Education Press).

RACK, P. H. (1976) 'Some Practical Problems in Providing a Psychiatric Service for Immigrants', presented at International Congress on Transcultural Psychiatry, Bradford.

RATTRAY, R. S. (1923) *Ashanti* (Oxford: Clarendon Press).

ROSE, E. J. B. (1969) *Colour and Citizenship* (Oxford University Press for Institute of Race Relations).

RUESCH, J. *et al.* (1948) 'Acculturation and Illness', *American Psychological Association Monograph* (Washington).

RUNNYMEDE TRUST (1975) 'Refugees: Their Status and Their Admission into the United Kingdom', *Briefing Paper No. 1/75* (London: Runnymede Trust).

—— (1977) 'Ethnic Minorities in Britain. A Select Bibliography', *Briefing Paper No. 6/77* (London: Runnymede.Trust).

SAIFULLAH KHAN, V. (1974) 'Pakistani Villages in a British City', unpublished Ph.D. thesis (Bradford University).

—— (1975) 'Asian Women in Britain: Strategies of Adjustment of Indian and Pakistani Migrants', in Alfred de Souza (ed.), *Women in Contemporary India* (Delhi: Manohar).

—— (1976a) 'Purdah in the British Situation', in D. L. Barker and S. Allen (eds), *Dependence and Exploitation in Work and Marriage* (London: Longmans).

—— (1976b) 'Pakistani Women in Britain', *New Community*, 5.

—— (1976c) 'Perceptions of a Population: Pakistanis in Britain', *New Community*, 5.

—— (1977) 'The Pakistanis: Mirpuri Villagers at Home and in the City of Bradford' in J. L. Watson (ed.), *Between Two Cultures: Migrants and Minorities in Britain* (Oxford: Blackwell).

—— (1979) 'Work and Network: South Asian Women in South London' in Sandra Wallman (ed.), *Ethnicity at Work* (London: Macmillan).

SCHOOLS COUNCIL (1967) *Working Paper 13: English for the Children of Immigrants* (London: HMSO).

SMITH, N. J., and McCulloch, W. (1976) 'Immigrants' Knowledge and Experience of Social Work Services', presented at International Congress on Transcultural Psychiatry, Bradford.

STEIN, H. F. (1975) 'Ethnicity, Identity, and Ideology', *School Review*, 83.

TAYLOR, J. H. (1976) *The Halfway Generation* (London: NFER Publishing Co.).

THOMAS, A., and SILLIN, S. (1972) *Racism and Psychiatry* (New York: Brunner/Mazel).

THOMPSON, M. (1974) 'The Second Generation – Punjabi or English' in *New Community*, vol. 3, no. 3.

TINKER, H. (1974) *The New System of Slavery* (Oxford University Press).

—— (1977) *The Banyan Tree: Overseas Emigrants from India, Pakistan and Bangladesh* (Oxford University Press).

TRAGER, H. G., and YARROW, M. R. (1952) *They Learn What They Live* (New York: Harper).

TRISELIOTIS, J. P. (ed.) (1972) *Social Work with Coloured Immigrants and Their Families* (Oxford University Press).

UCHENDU, V. C. (1965) *The Igbo of Southeast Nigeria* (New York: Holt, Rienhart and Winston).

VALENTINE, C. (1968) *Culture and Poverty* (University of Chicago Press).

VATUK, S. (1972) *Kinship and Urbanisation: White-collar Migrants in North India* (London: University of California Press).

WATSON, J. L. (ed.) (1977) *Between Two Cultures: Migrants and Minorities in Britain* (Oxford: Blackwell).

WEINREICH, P. (1975a) 'Conflicts in Identity and the Perception of Ethnic Groups', Mimeographed report available from the SSRC Research Unit on Ethnic Relations at the University of Bristol, Bristol, England.

—— (1975b) 'Identity Diffusion in Immigrant and English Adolescents', paper read to the British Psychological Society's Annual Conference at Nottingham, and published in 1979 in G. K. Verma and C. Bagley (eds), *Race, Education and Identity* (London: Macmillan).

WEISS, M. S. (1970) 'Selective Acculturation and the Dating Process: The Patterning of Chinese – Caucasian Interracial Dating', *Journal of Marriage and the Family*, 32.

WORLD HEALTH ORGANISATION (1974) *The International Pilot Study of Schizophrenia* (Geneva: World Health Organisation).

Index